I0308561

Also by Lee Israel

ESTÉE LAUDER: BEYOND THE MAGIC

KILGALLEN

MISS TALLULAH BANKHEAD

Can You Ever Forgive Me?

Memoirs of a Literary Forger

LEE ISRAEL

Simon & Schuster Paperbacks

NEW YORK   LONDON   TORONTO   SYDNEY   NEW DELHI

SIMON & SCHUSTER PAPERBACKS
An Imprint of Simon & Schuster, Inc.
1230 Avenue of the Americas
New York, NY 10020

This Simon & Schuster trade paperback edition October 2018

The characteristics of some individuals and chronology of
some events have been changed.

For information about special discounts for bulk purchases, please contact
Simon & Schuster Special Sales at 1-866-506-1949
or business@simonandschuster.com.

Designed by C. Linda Dingler

Printed and bound by CPI Group (UK) Ltd, Croydon, CR0 4YY

1   2   3   4   5   6   7   8   9   10

Library of Congress Cataloging-in-Publication Data

Israel, Lee.
Can you ever forgive me? : memoirs of a literary forger / Lee Israel.
        p. cm.
1. Israel, Lee. 2. Forgers—United States—Biography.
3. Literary forgeries and mystifications. 4. Letters—Forgeries. I. Title.
PN171.F6I77   2008
364.16'3—dc22   2008022495

ISBN 978-1-9821-1689-7 (pbk)
ISBN 978-1-9821-1760-3 (ebook)

For Bill Aue . . . who would have had fun

with all this . . .

and Byron Dobell

Contents

CONTENTS

Can You Ever Forgive Me?

They were such good company, even by letter. My pet was Dorothy Parker. When the correspondence began in 1962 she had just moved out of her digs at the Hotel Volney in New York to settle in West Hollywood with her husband, Alan Campbell. A letter to her friend Germaine about the move:

DOROTHY PARKER
8983 NORMA PLACE
HOLLYWOOD, CALIFORNIA

January 27, 1962

Dear Germaine,

        Please be sure to change my
mailing address to the above. Your letters
are a comfort and I would hate missing them.
There are several review copies that I never
received.

        The old address, which you will
now disregard, is the Hotel Volney, 23 East
74th, New York City. I tell you that for XXX
history's sake or in case your files are vertical.

        Gertrude Stein was right about
roses, but she was all wet about California.
She said there was "no there there." Well,
I'm here to tell you there is.

        If Alan were home (about the most
conditional sentence I have ever composed),
he would send enormous love and best regards.

        Yours,

Dorothy Parker

P.S. I have a hangover out of Gounod's _Faust_.

My special circle included Edna Ferber, one of the most popular and prolific writers of her time—a scold, a snob, a low-profile dominatrix whose corseted asperity was never far from busting out. If Ferber hadn't gone from small-town reporter to big-time writer, she would doubtless have had a rocky but enduring Boston marriage and ended her days as dean of one of the elite women's colleges, where she would have been talked about plenty.

She hated noise and did not take kindly to criticism. Here she is at her most Ferberly, omitting a salutation and addressing someone we can only know as "thoughtful boy":

I loved your flowers,thoughtful boy. They were waiting
impatiently for me when I returned from Main Chance.
It was just the lift I needed after returning home to
a major construction job in progress right outside my
apartment. These workmen,with their foul language and
their coarse hollering will make a Tory of me yet.

I thought about the idea of your approaching La Hepburn
and I don't think this is the best time. I spoke with
her last week. The Kramer film is on schedule, but
very taxing to Spence. He has no residual energy and
is even crankier than usual, which is very cranky
indeed. Kate said that he has just about every major
ailment associated with aging. She is trying to keep
her remarkable chin up but the situation is very touch-
and-go. All their energies are concentrated now on
finishing the picture. Kramer is shooting in sequence
and he's got to do a six-page,very powerful,absolutely
crucial scene any day now.She was near to tears.Not the
Kate I know and have known for decades.Give her time.
She has nothing left over.

I gather you didn't like the book.That is your privilege.
I do.As a matter of fact,dear heart,I've liked just
about everything I've ever written, and that is how I
muster the stuff to get to my machine every day--
in spite of the conspiracy of noise from a hostile
bloc of blue-collar s with jackhammers from hell.
Tomorrow,I'll pray for rain.

    I love you.

                    Herb.

Louise Brooks, the left-hemispheric actress turned essayist and critic, a fabulous creature—literate, passionate, bitter as a root, a great destroyer of Hollywood myth, and an Olympian hater—was, in the time period represented by her correspondence, spending the last years of her life in a modest Rochester, New York, apartment, subsisting on a straitening stipend paid to her every month by ex-boyfriend William F. Paley, her legend among cineastes swelling like popcorn, though her iconic raven pageboy had morphed into a salt-and-pepper topknot.

Here she is writing to "Dorothy," extruding a great deal of venom on paterfamilias Joseph Kennedy:

7 North Goodman St - Rochester NY - 14607

Dear Dorothy

My "source" for most of what we spoke about, in
addition to my own experiences with George Marshall,
was John Springer. You know that he was Monroe's publicity
agent and a constant, longtime friend of mine.

That terrible old fart, the Tyranny Adict Joe Kennedy,
ruined Gloria Swanson by luring her away from Paramount
and then dumping her uncerimoniously. He established a
foothold out there and presented the town to his boys as
their well-stocked and private whore house. They had to
have beautiful Marilyn. She became even more headily
wayward with regard to her film career, assuming that her
closeness to their redoubtable power would make it all
right with Fox. She was "told" that it would be all right
with Fox. Then she took her little hideaway house, but
nobody came to protect her or make it all right. There
were finally only subpoena servers from Fox. She could
have compelled the protection she so poignantly needed by
threatening those beasts with disclosing that she had laid
the President and the Attorney General. She did not have
the guile or the stomach for such blood sport and so she took
pills instead.

The dignified Joe di Maggio had the guts and grace
to bar Bobby from her funeral! I hate the Kennedys.
Their goal was to lay all the beauties in Babylon and
their carelessness and cruelty--taught to them by a
father with the instincts of a vicious beast--resulted
in the rubbling of a delicate and decent woman. She was
one of many victims.

I know you will like the "young" essays of Virginia
Woolf but beware. She is totally deluded about her parents.
Those abominations , had they lived longer, would have
stuck her in a loony bin with her sister. And I suspect
that would happen to me if I ever decided to countermand
Thomas Wolfe's injunction. Wichita has been spoiling for
my ass since XXXXXXXXXXXXXXXXXXXXXXXXXXXXXXXXXXXXX Hector
was a Plains Indian.

                    Regards

                              Louise-
                              Brooks

There was endless wit from dear Noël Coward, writing a great deal about his friends and the leading ladies on whom he blamed everything, including his wayward diverticulum. Marlene Dietrich was his dearest and, with the possible exception of Clifton Webb, his most annoying friend.

Sunday.

Dear Boy,

        The London sojourn was
exhausting.   Marlene's opening was
divine.   The silly old Kraut remains
one of the most attractive women on the
face of the earth and during this brief
period of triumph has ceased moaning about
getting old.   As I have told you on
countless occasions I am sure--Marlene
seems to think that she is the only higher
primate to suffer the depradations of growing and she is determinedly ungraceful
about the whole business.

old
V

        Are you tired yet of
of my paeans to the Queen Mother.   We
all watched "Ninety Years On" together.
She was moved and I was thrilled.   I
love her more and more for her good heart
and her grand style.   That she is
genuinely fond of me delights me beyond
my meagre powers of expression.

        You told me nothing about
Bob.   Am I to assume that it is over?

        Yours, as ever,

Brick and Pigeons

*I*f with that last letter you pictured the urbane playwright in Switzerland, cigarette-holdered and smoking-jacketed, dashing off a letter in the 1960s from a cozy nook high up in Chalet Coward—the house he bought in the Alps to take advantage of Switzerland's kinda gentler tax laws—located at Les Avants, Montreux, just down the mountain from the David Nivens at Château d'Oex, where Coward entertained guests that included Marlene, Garbo, George Cukor, Rebecca West, and a group that Elaine Stritch once called "all the Dames Edith" . . . you would be wrong.

Every letter reproduced here, along with hundreds like them, were turned out by me—conceived, written, typed, and signed—in my perilously held studio apartment in the shadow of Zabar's on New York's Upper West Side in 1991 and 1992. A room with a view not of Alpine splendor, but of brick and pigeons, a modest flat I took in the spring of 1969 with the seventy-five-hundred-dollar advance that G. P. Putnam's Sons had given me to do my first book, a biography of Tallulah Bankhead. I sold those letters to various autograph dealers, first in New York City, and was soon branching out across the country and abroad—for seventy-five dollars a pop.

Noël Coward's soi-disant letters were typed by me on what I remember was a 1950ish Olympia manual, solid as a rock, bigger than a bread box, not so much portable as luggable. (Noël's Olympia was the one I would have the most trouble schlepping when the FBI was about to come calling.) For the nonce, I was content, researching my Tallulah bio—just me, my cat, and my contract, in my cozy, rent-controlled room-with-no-view.

I had never known anything but "up" in my career, had never received even one of those formatted no-thank-you slips that successful writers look back upon with triumphant jocularity. And I regarded with pity and disdain the short-sleeved wage slaves who worked in offices. I had no reason to believe life would get anything but better. I had had no experience failing.

Miss Tallulah Bankhead was a succès d'estime. The book had respectable sales and attracted many admirers, especially in the gay community. (By which I mean men. Lesbians don't seem to harbor the gay sensibility with the same vigorous attention to detail as the guys who, I suspect, are born with the Great American Songbook clinging to the walls of their Y chromosomes.) I continued to be wined and wooed by publishers, in various venues of young veal and Beefeater gin. My second book, *Kilgallen,* was conceived at one of those chic, deductible lunches, over gorgeous gin martinis. My work on the book began in the mid-1970s and continued for about four years.

I researched at the Library for the Performing Arts at Lincoln Center, where I was always comfortable. (I had even given the library a percentage of my take on *Tallulah*.) *Kilgallen* sold well and made the best-seller list of *The New York Times*. It appeared for one week with a snippy little commentary by the book-section editor, running as a kind of footer—the commentary, not the editor. Since I had written for the Arts and Leisure section frequently, when it was under the talented editorship of Seymour Peck, the paper's distaste for my work surprised and chagrined. No matter. I was now entitled to say that I was a *New York Times* best-selling author, and I frequently did. A particularly compelling part of the Kilgallen story was her controversial death, which had occurred just after she told friends that she was about to reveal the truth about the assassination of JFK. I remember swimming laps, with the mantra "Who killed Dorothy? Who killed Dorothy?" playing under my swim cap. I made money from my second book. Not Kitty Kelley, beachfront-property money, and no more than I would have made in four years in middle management at a major corporation . . . as if any major corporation would have had me, or I it. There was enough, however, to keep me in restaurants and taxis.

Wretched and Excessive

I was imprudent with money and Dionysian to the quick. Having worked so long and hard on the last book, I took many months off to play. I fell in love with a brilliant, beautiful bartender named Elaine, a lapsed Catholic who now observed only Bloomsday and St. Patrick's—the first with solemnity, the latter with wretched excess. And so I took more time to play.

There were several false starts on various projects, which meant months of research, working on a particular book only to find that there was no book there. Not my kind of book. I had to abandon Judy Holliday, Bette Davis (she wanted me to co-author one of her several autobiographies, and when people asked me what had finally gone wrong with the project, I told them "I yelled back!"), Roy Cohn, Vanessa Redgrave, and Woody Allen. Of course, advances had to be returned, and in their entirety, though many thousands had been spent by me in determining that a book was not doable. Writers, unlike lawyers, doctors, agents, and Verizon Information, do not get paid when they fail or misjudge.

Just as I was down to the last five hundred of my remaining IRA, along came Estée Lauder, the colossus of fragrance and cosmetics, about whom Macmillan wanted an unauthorized biography—warts and all. I accepted the offer though I didn't give a shit about her warts. I needed the money badly. Macmillan paid in the high five figures.

Before I could say "gift with purchase," I was made another offer *not* to treat Estée's warts. The counteroffer came from Estée herself through the late and unlamented attorney Roy Cohn, with a man named Lou Katz acting as intermediary and bag man in the wings. (In 2002 Katz would be extradited from Panama, where he had fled after being convicted of the murder of the new lover of his old boyfriend. He had been free for thirteen years before his capture.) He communicated with me through a mutual friend, Jack Hock, who had worked for him when Katz owned a gay bar called Uncle Charlie's . . . which had seemed to me, on my several visits, not the *least* bit avuncular. The first offer from Estée-Cohn-Katz was $60,000—enough to settle the back taxes I owed the feds and to return an advance I had previously been paid to do a job on Roy Cohn himself.

I was not the first writer assigned to Estée Lauder. *New York Post* columnist Cindy Adams recounted at the time of Estée's death at ninety-seven that she had once undertaken such a book and been leaned on by Roy Cohn to drop the project. "I was parrying," she wrote in 2004, "with the smartest and the toughest." Adams finally abandoned the work in progress when other assignments came her way. When I chose to parry back and refused the sixty-thousand-dollar inducement, Katz, who resembled a seedy Barry Manilow, left Jack Hock the message, "Tell Lee that the old lady says she can name her price." I didn't like or even trust the offer and issued a final refusal. Perhaps I'd seen too many Gregory Peck films in my impressionable years—Peck with his simmering projections of outraged probity—and emerged from the exposures with the opinion that taking bribes was wrong. So I did the book for Macmillan. It was rushed out because Estée, ever the competitor, was racing to market with her own putative life story, in which she admitted finally to being Jewish!

My book was keenly anticipated by Doubleday's flagship store in New York City, which was right across the street from the headquarters of both Lauder and Revlon. So of course a good deal of interest was evinced at the store by the employees of both firms about my unauthorized *Estée Lauder: Beyond the Magic*. Based on the interest shown, the store assumed that my book would have legs like a brace of centipedes. I pre-signed more than a hundred copies. The book did okay there on account of all the cosmetics people who knew that Estée had much that she kept hidden about her old-time religion; it turned out, however, that the secret stuff just wasn't that secret. She had not fooled too many people when, for instance, she talked tendentiously about her brunches in Palm Beach "every Sunday after church." I was pleased to sign all those copies for the Doubleday store, but not so pleased when I returned to find that many of my autographed books were still on the shelf—where I would join them straightaway.

I had made a mistake. Instead of taking a great deal of money from a woman rich as Oprah, I published a bad, unimportant book, rushed out in months to beat the other little piggy to market. The reviews were not good. Sales were poor. The Estée Lauder biography was the beginning of the end for me as a hotshot writer. I'd left my cake out in the rain. No more two-martini wooing at the Four Seasons.

And I blame Gregory Peck!

A Mayan Minute

*O*ver a period of about three years, I plummeted from best-sellerdom to welfare, with a couple of pit stops in between. I had adored the writing life and the freedom that accompanied it. I never took it absolutely for granted, but I assumed that if anything happened I could strike a tolerable bargain by taking to the marketplace the segregable skills I had developed in decades of researching and writing nonfiction. This turned out not to be the case. The marketplace has no little box called "book writer." I had not done time in the pillory. I hadn't worked at a real *job*.

That I was "rising" fifty years old (one of Noël's favorite words) further hindered. Nor did it help that the personality

I had developed—working at home with a cat on my lap, being told at the martini'd lunches how very good I was—was rather outsized. Yet I needed to work in order to survive.

The employment agent who sent me out described the job as fund-raising for a foundation. The foundation turned out to be the private bailiwick of a very rich and unpleasant woman who spent a great deal of time traipsing after and scrutinizing the spoor of mountain gorillas in Rwanda. Her foundation worked on behalf of these great apes and I assumed the job would be related to them. As it turned out, however, I was to function as one of two personal assistants to her, working out of her behemoth Sutton Place apartment, full of pre-Columbian oddments, where two nervous Chinese domestics functioned in servile service.

My responsibilities included ordering food from the grocery for her and the family, reserving limos for evenings out with her eye-candy husband, and answering her telephone. The telephonic salutation was to include her long and difficult last name. I never quite mastered Rich Lady's moniker, which tripped on my tongue rather than off it. Then there was a log thing. I was instructed to write entries in this log to account for every minute of my time on the job.

We worked in cramped quarters without any space that had been genuinely allocated, so when Ruth Truly came into the so-called office it was necessary for one of us to rise and give her a seat. The other assistant, very young and sweet, wore a large picture hat like Virginia Hill, the mob tootsie who testified at the Kefauver crime hearings a very long time ago. She filled out her log agreeably, writing, vis-à-vis her downtime, jottings like: "3:00–3:30, practiced my typing"; "3:30–4:00, worked on improving my handwriting." Four-thirty to five? Picked a bale of cotton.

Presently, my-lady-of-the-gorilla-spoor told me that one of my duties would be balancing the checkbooks of her perfectly hideous teenagers. I bristled. Was I now to play Eve Arden to these monstrous teens? The session turned into an evaluation. Rich Lady brought up the matter of the personal log that was still tabula rasa, and opined that I didn't seem to be "fitting in." I thanked her for noticing just as one of the Chinese domestics was beckoned to show me to the door of the plantation, doubtless to make sure that I did not pocket one of the pre-Columbian arrowheads—which I would have done in a Mayan minute. I'd lasted four days.

I began taking "temp" assignments as a legal proofreader at various elite law firms in New York City, working typically on the graveyard shift, where the sun don't shine, but the pay is better. The work was done in a bare monkish cubbyhole, no telephone, surrounded by what seemed like oak tag on three sides of me. My tools were a six-inch ruler—the kind we used in third grade—and four sharpened No. 2 pencils.

In the monkish cell, I proofread and "blacklined" lawyers' briefs. Working side by side among other monks, all in a row, I was given two versions of a brief—an early and an emended later version. Using carets and straight lines, my blacklining was intended to show what changes had been made to the document as it progressed through various stages. The blacklining established a chain of change and imputed responsibility: where, for instance, "company owned" was deleted from one version and turned by some rash attorney into "company held." Heads might roll.

I earned maybe nineteen dollars an hour, waiting agonized for the dawn, when the muscular New York skyline would emerge from behind its scrim and manumit me. Many of these assignments came from one agency owner, who told me that she had changed her last name from Slaughter to Laughter, by blacklining her *S*. She, too, was coming to the conclusion that I was not quite up to snuff, and advised me to study the behavior of the veteran legal proofreaders with whom I shared my shifts. There was something in my personality that was rubbing her clients the wrong way. Clearly, she meant a little more Dickens, and a lot less Saroyan,

. . .

I supplemented my meager income by selling some of the books that lined my studio apartment. I took them serially to the Strand Book Store on lower Broadway. The Strand was the last resort when I was down to my last five or six dollars. At the Strand, there was a tall, reedy man with all the warmth of Dick Cheney, who did the buying. I'd had what must have been thirty or forty transactions with him, and he never once greeted me. It seemed not to have occurred to him that the people selling their cherished volumes were the backbone of his business. One fine day, I left my apartment with a touch of arthritis, an armful of books, and just enough money for a one-way trip downtown. I wasn't worried. I had learned enough about secondhand books to expect at least eight dollars for the lot.

He was more glacial than ever that day; he glanced at the pile and said, "Not interested. Take them to Fourth Avenue, maybe they'll give you something." I was familiar with his buying proclivities by that point and realized that he was pulling a major power trip on me. But as I began to gather up the books I also knew that I just could not carry my load any farther. I walked away, leaving the books on his counter, hoping to borrow some money from a friend nearby in the West Village. The Strand Man said, "Hey, get your garbage off my counter!" There followed some exchange. I'm certain that the words *glacial, merchant,* and *prick* issued from my mouth, and probably *Pickwickian* as well. It's my pre-tears word, never bothered to look it up. And then . . . with a glorious Ruthian swing, I swept the load of hefty books off the counter onto his wooden floor. Whereupon I was 86'd from the Strand, one of my last sources of disposable income.

I tried selling what was left of my library on the street, rolling the bridge table that had been in the family forever, on which not a trick of bridge was to my knowledge ever played (though my grandmother told me that she and "Sylvia Sidney's mother" had once played cards together, she never specified the game), to a kind of peddlers' row, a stone's throw away from my Riverside Drive apartment. I sold the books for a couple of dollars apiece, turning around from the red table and wheeling myself into the gutter whenever I spied approaching neighbors. There, to keep them from knowing the dire state of my economy, I waved my arms and pretended to be hailing a taxi.

I went on and off welfare, a horror beyond my talent to describe. My most enduring memory is the odor in the elevators: eau de desperation! I was hag-ridden with worry about landing on the street, and I was not in the flower of mental health, drinking quite a bit and doing mischief when drunk.

I footered over the treatment I'd received at the Strand,

which, to paraphrase Dorothy Parker, had involved more than one bastard. The Strand Man had a younger version of himself at his left side as he inspected and offered piratical prices for the secondhand books brought to the store. The younger man looked just like him. Could have been a son. On the day of the ugly episode, the guy I'll call Little Strand Man had escorted me to the exit and instructed the store guards: "She's not allowed back in the Strand *ever!*"

The bookstore episode had occurred perhaps two weeks before Christmas. On Christmas Day, in a bright wintry light, I was on my way to a ham dinner with some friends on Central Park West when I espied Little Strand Man exit his smallish apartment house, looking lonely as a cloud, his only companion an adorable brown puppy, obviously worshipped, at the end of an expensive leash. As the duo disappeared up the street, I entered the building's foyer and copied down the names of a few of his neighbors.

On what I remember was the very next day, I trained downtown to the Strand's environs. There I found a public phone with a good view of the store. I telephoned the Strand and asked for "the young man," identifying myself as one of his neighbors. He came to the phone. I said, "There's a fire in our building. I just got my two cats out. But the firemen are not going in for the animals."

In seconds, the panicked book clerk, trying to negotiate

the second sleeve of his crummy coat, came running out of the Strand's front door, catching the first available taxi. There was no fire, of course, no reluctant firefighters . . . just one agonized Strand employee beginning a hellish trip uptown.

The rest of the capers were less malicious; they invariably involved the telephone. The AA crowd calls it "drinking and dialing." A plethora of people had ceased to return my calls—important people in publishing and media. Loaded up, usually on gin, and adoring my own larkiness, I'd telephone somebody who was once my buddy but was now in "meetings" all the time. I'd make a second call, with just a slight change in attitude and voice, identifying myself often as Nora Ephron. The erstwhile conferee would come on in a trice, usually with a warm "Hiya, Nora," whereupon I shouted "Star fucker! Is that one word or two?" and hung up. Once I pretended to be Barbra Streisand's secretary, calling Esther Newberg, a titan among agents and a real tough broad. Her secretary answered, and I looked forward to a secretarial pissing contest as Newberg's assistant asked me to hold. It took about two minutes; a breathless, pre-cardiac Newberg came finally to the phone. I told her she had *just* missed Ms. Streisand, on her way to Rwanda in search of gorilla spoor. I had never even met Esther Newberg, but I knew she wouldn't have taken a call from Lee Israel. Besides, it was raining.

Eventually I received a letter from Ephron's lawyer; then two detectives came to my apartment. They used words like *harassment*. "Well," I said, "if she can't take a joke . . ." I promised to cease and also desist, but knew the impulsivity that gin induces would inevitably chivy me to the telephone. Fortunately, it was disconnected for nonpayment before I could get myself into serious trouble.

The Flies

The flies were the beginning of the end. They appeared in early 1990, an Upper West Side anomaly, something like a registered Republican. Upper West Siders do not get flies, they get roaches. And I had no idea where my critters were coming from. For days, I thought there was just one busy little fly; then I saw them all in a black bunch, lined up across two or three slats of my cheap and dusty venetians—like the crows in Hitchcock.

When I think back I realize that I must have been having some kind of breakdown. The cause of the flies couldn't have been more obvious, but I remained oblivious to the connection: my twenty-one-year-old cat, Jersey, infirm and addled with age. The darling spent almost all of her time under my bed; nothing interested her anymore—not catnip, not even mousey. She appeared infrequently for a little water and a dollop of food but she had begun to disappear behind her eyes, in the way of dying animals, and her litter box remained almost pristine. I heard her only once or twice, her back legs stiffened with age, clopping about pathetically, sounding like she was wearing wooden shoes. I would have taken her to every specialist in New York had I any money, but I made peace with what the neighborhood vet told me: she was in no pain and she would very soon pass, probably in her sleep.

Yet I found no connection between the flies and my Jersey's litter box, though it should have been clear that she was doing what my Grandma Lena used to call her "business" under my bed, and her business was attracting flies. I did not smell anything; rather like those serial killers who garnish their flats with hacked-off human parts but never seem bothered by or even aware of the stench.

I tried swatting the flies; couldn't make a dent. For Jersey's sake, I avoided store-bought insecticides. Then I remembered a local Chinese take-out place that specialized in cheap and terrific fried chicken, which I ordered at least twice a week. For a time I had avoided the restaurant because I saw too many common houseflies there. Presently, they seemed to be all gone, disappeared. Now I asked the nice Chinese lady in charge what she had done to banish the buzzers. She understood English far better than she could speak it. And she said repeatedly something I just couldn't understand. Patiently, she tore off a piece of one of her menus, pointed to the hardware store across the street, and wrote in blunt pencil: FRY PAPER.

I bought three packages of TAT, four tubes to a package, which depicted dead flies promisingly, upside-down and plainly dead. I unfurled all the rolls when I returned home, tacking them up around the apartment. The sticky stuff to which the flies were supposed to adhere was all over my hands and all over the walls. I stuck to each of the rolls, and in extricating myself pulled on the live-looking glops so that they curled up and over, like the crest of a wave about to break. With my moribund cat thumping around from time to time, TAT waves over every surface, the apartment looked more and more like the set of *Little Shop of Horrors*. But there was no relief from the flies. One or two did what they were supposed to do and adhered to the glop on the flypaper; many more died collaterally by my windows, obviously concussed in a valiant effort to flee my flat.

Owing back rent, I was shy about asking the building management for anything, but I did eventually go to the phone on the corner to let the landlord know that I needed an exterminator. Management promised to send one the next day. That day, as I returned from the check-cashing store where I picked up food stamps, I encountered my superintendent, Mr. Colon, who told me that the exterminator had been there. "Great. Those flies were driving me nuts," I said. Mr. Colon continued. The exterminator had come, taken one look at the state of my apartment, and refused to enter it.

Can you have a wake-up call without a telephone?

Slippery Slope

There was a time when, for me, *Soap Opera Digest* would have been infra dig. Now I was writing an occasional piece for the magazine about old-time radio soaps like *Ma Perkins.* The money was minimal; the articles, however, were fun. I did most of my research at the Library for the Performing Arts at Lincoln Center, where one day I requested material about Elaine Carrington, a big-deal soap writer of her time, thinking there might be material for a story in her papers. I was given a box with various folders inside, one of them containing a clutch of letters from Fanny Brice to Carrington. The content was unextraordinary. Fanny apparently saved the good stuff for face-to-face meetings. As she said in a genuine letter: "Everything is grand, will tell you lots and lots when I see you. . . . I am a much better actress than a writer so I can act it out for you." All the letters were typed on Fanny's note-sized and personalized stationery.

I was working in the large readers' room that accommodates the general public. I should not have been given the box there. Material of value—and a note signed by Fanny Brice had some value—was reposited as a rule in the smaller, more secure Katharine Cornell Room.

Thinking of celebrity letters as saleable things rather than primary sources of information was new to me. In my past, I had owned and sold only one such: a poignant, handwritten letter from Katharine Hepburn to me, all about Spencer Tracy's death, on the same day he and Hepburn were to have posed for the cover of *Esquire* magazine. I had received Hepburn's letter soon after I met her while covering her return to acting in *Guess Who's Coming to Dinner* for *Esquire,* assigned to me by Byron Dobell, a prince among editors. The ink in the handwritten letter was splotched in places, as though by moisture—a condition for which Hepburn apologized: "all tears," she wrote. I kept it, of course, and rather cherished it. When my career began to snap into reverse (a court officer would later describe that period as a "tough patch") I sold the letter to a great New York character named Anna Sosenko. Anna was in her early eighties when I met her after venturing into her basement shop in the West Seventies or Eighties, a square, squat dumpling of a woman who looked like one of those aging sopranos given to wearing long capes. She bought and sold autographs and high-end memorabilia there; in addition, she knew everyone in New York and produced fund-raising galas. I learned that she had discovered and virtually created the career of "the incomparable" Hildegarde, the swank cabaret singer, and that she had written the standard "Darling, Je Vous Aime Beaucoup," while the two were still speaking to each other. Anna paid me $250 for the letter, which I needed more than I needed Hepburn's tears.

At the time I was riffling through the Fanny Brice letters, I had recently found Doris, a gorgeous tortoiseshell kitten with a face half burnt orange and half black. (I named her after an ex-lover, who was also two-faced and from a large litter.) My ancient and ailing Jersey had died peacefully in her sleep some weeks before. I had scrubbed her area and witnessed the mass migration of the flies. Given my awful penury, I would never have taken another cat, but Doris was practically a gift from the gods . . . which is to say that I found her in the street, peeking out from behind the curbside front tire of a parked car, and calling to me. How to resist? Alas, she had begun to refuse food and the fast was taking her into a danger zone. Unlike Mohandas Gandhi, felines can't stop eating and expect a visit from Candice Bergen; they do themselves mortal damage if the fast lasts too long. I had come up with forty dollars for her first vet's visit, but did not have the additional seventy-five without which Dr. Moses would not perform some diagnostic tests. I didn't have the money for the tests and I could not borrow it. I had never drawn any crowds, but my drinking and moaning, the magnet of my mini fame enfeebled, my antic behavior—all repelled the few friends I'd had. And Moses was no longer amused by Israel's promise to give up worshipping false idols if he'd treat her animals on credit.

So I stole three Fanny Brice letters, slid them into a small notebook, ducked into the ladies' room, and planted them gingerly between my socks and my Keds. I chattered nervously as I passed through the perfunctory inspection of two library guards, and hit the streets in search of the Yellow Pages.

Remember the hysterical laughing and hollering and banjo-backed whoop-de-doos as the hotly pursued Bonnie and Clyde gang crossed the state line into Oklahoma? There was a lot of that kind of exultation and relief in me as I exited Lincoln Center, removing myself and my pelf from harm's way. I felt no guilt about the letters. They were from the realm of the dead. Doris and I were alive and well and living on the West Side.

There was no shortage of autograph dealers in New York: Argosy, Autographs by Gary Combs, Cambridge-Essex, Lion Heart, Kenneth R. Rendell Gallery, Tollet and Harmon, and David Schulson were among them. "We've been buying and selling since 1887," "Anxious to purchase small or large collections," "Religious content wanted." (Have I got a shroud for you!) I chose and telephoned the most conveniently located, the Argosy Book Store, just across the park from Lincoln Center. Yes, there was interest in Fanny Brice. Naomi Hample asked me to come right over.

Cousin Sidney

I opted to walk through the park, eastward along the narrow walkway beside the constant, rumbling traffic. The walk gave me time to think about "provenance," one of the principal considerations in judging the authenticity of an artifact. In a high wind of creativity, I invented Cousin Sidney Brozen. My mother had actually had a cousin so named, who with his wife, Estelle, had owned a jewelry store in the East Seventies before they joined the early-bird raptors in Florida. My fictional Sidney was, or had been, an independently wealthy and well-connected world traveler always with the carnation in his lapel, who had lived among and cultivated the great and the glamorous. He'd adored outsized personalities and, decades before his death, I would claim, began saving their letters and collecting others. I would tell the dealers that Sidney had bequeathed me his entire epistolary canon—a trove of autographed letters for me to handle, with minor exceptions, as I saw fit. I could keep them, sell them, perhaps make use of them from time to time in a book. I had made a deathbed promise to him, however: I would under no circumstances part with the correspondence of his "tormented sopranos," Maria Callas and Rosa Ponselle, whom Sidney was determined to protect from unseemly scrutiny. By the time I reached Fifth Avenue, I realized that I was imagining a kind of Jewish James Caan . . . aesthete, opera queen, boulevardier, my boutonniered benefactor.

I reached Argosy on Fifty-ninth Street, a six-story building tucked between skyscrapers. Naomi Hample was paged from her sixth-floor office down to the first. She was an attractive woman, early forties, not tall, what used to be called short-waisted. As I remember, she was wearing a brown wool suit to complement her reddish hair. Her deep voice had an attractive caught-cold quality.

I would learn that she was one of the three daughters of the store's founder, Louis Cohen, who had started small on Fourth Avenue more than sixty years before, working his way uptown to Bloomingdale's country. He had been astute enough to buy the building in which his middle daughter and I now sat, at a large mahogany table, its corners layered with doubtlessly valuable clutter.

Hample, in a pair of large, owlish glasses, read the Brice letters, rather quickly I thought. She looked up and asked me whether I was *the* Lee Israel, which was half the battle. I began telling her about Sidney, but she evinced no great interest in coz. She offered and I accepted what I recall was forty dollars apiece for three letters, explaining that she would pay more for better content. I rode home in a taxi, jingle in my jeans. Adding to the jubilation, Doris, without the benefit of veterinary intervention, had licked her platter clean. Banjos, please!

I bought the first of a long and distinguished line of manual typewriters: a clattery, jet-black Royal, old enough to have been used by Fanny or, more likely, her secretary, from my neighborhood hardware store where various secondhand items were—still are—put on the street for quick sale: chipped china, worthless books, and old typewriters, the last singing siren songs to passing Upper West Siders nostalgic for the clatter of typing . . . as opposed to the silence of keyboarding.

After I tapped out my own message, something like "Now is the time for Funny Girl to come to the aid of Lee Israel," to determine that the stygian black portable worked when worked upon, had a ribbon that turned on its own, and a pica typeface similar to Fanny's, I paid the man thirty dollars and took the venerable Royal home in its hard tan case.

I went back to the library for more Fanny Brice notes. I jazzed them up in my apartment later with Hample's words about good content in mind. There was plenty of room under the body of the letters for postscripts. In one that I typed, Fanny was made to say something about Nicky Arnstein. She had divorced him in 1927, way before the date of the letter, but the mere mention of the gambler who had figured so prominently in the Streisand biopic would add, I estimated, another twenty or thirty dollars to the value of the letter.

While writing this memoir, I made a few attempts to recover or at least determine the whereabouts of some of my original letters. I had sent copies of most of them to my mother and stepfather in Florida, who hadn't a clue about the situation. I instructed them to put them all in some safe place. For reasons now lost to me, the Fanny Brice copies were not dispatched to Florida. I could find nothing of her, not originals or copies. In looking for them, I tried telephoning various dealers, many of whom I'd worked with the decade before, assuming they would not recognize my disguised voice. The pitch started: "Hello, this is Leonore

Louise

The idea of growing my newfound vocation came with the discovery of a luscious collection . . . more than 150 long letters, "TLSs" (typed letters signed), written by Louise Brooks from Rochester, New York, to her friend, film archivist Herman G. Weinberg. Louise's letters were done between December 1962, when she was fifty-six and beginning an enormously satisfying literary career, and October 1983, by which point she was suffering from emphysema and osteoarthritis and unable to type.

The Lincoln Center library gave me a lot less latitude here than I'd had with the Fanny Brice material. No duplicating was permitted. Nor were pens permissible. I sat now in the relatively secure Katharine Cornell Room (which has since been made a lot more secure), taking extensive notes from the letters, most of which had been typed by Louise on plain paper. She used an assortment of hot-colored pencils—orange, red, and purple—to underline violently and to sign her name. Getting through the collection took weeks of assiduous attention, but by the time I had read all the letters, most of which ran to about three hundred words, I had a nook-and-cranny familiarity with the passionate Louise Brooks, silent-film star turned cranky, iconoclastic critic of movies, movie stars, and Hollywood hagiography.

None of my forgeries were to my knowledge ever subjected to any kind of scientific testing. But common sense dictated that I needed older-looking paper for the Louise Brooks canon. Most of the happy surprises at the library I discovered, to the vast annoyance of the burly "box boy" who fetched my multiple requests, by rummaging through odd lots of old material. One of the best discoveries was in the papers of Mady Christians, the distinguished Austrian-born actress known for creating the title character onstage in John van Druten's *I Remember Mama.* Christians's papers contained notes for a class she was teaching at Columbia University—all gathered in bulky loose-leaf books. (She had been rendered unemployable as an actress after being targeted in one of the Communist witch-hunts of the McCarthy era.) At the back of each of the binders I discovered a plenitude of off-white, beautifully weathered paper. Perfect canvases for the letters of Louise. The holes hardly mattered. Louise could have used punctured paper. I grabbed a generous supply and passed easily through the guards. I was carrying, after all, just some blank paper.

Obtaining persuasive writing paper for those subjects who used personalized stationery had been a cinch. I simply took a sample of the letterhead that I had duplicated at the library, brought it to a printer, and had it multiply copied. I was amused to be called Miss Hellman by one printer, and Mrs. Ferber by another. Signatures, however, would require artful practice. At the library and most surreptitiously I'd traced several of Louise's signatures through the lightest-weight paper I could buy. Back home, seated at my desk, I experimented. First, I tried copying side by side—an original traced signature to my left, the weathered blank canvases at my right. Slowly and so painstakingly I tried to imitate the tortuous course of Louise's flamboyant chirography. No good! Then I tried tracing over the various signature samples I had taken, weathered paper on top of the signatures. The problem here was exacerbated by my inability to *see* the original through the marvelously time-tainted but heavily weighted paper. Again, my attempts flopped. The work was a poster child for signature fakery—just crying out for some dealer's *gotcha!* and manifesting clearly what the experts call "forgers' palsy." I could have qualified for a telethon. My signatures were shaky, uneven, a trail of lifted pencils and muscular betrayal. Shit!

Riffing

Then I invented the light box. Or thought I had. I owned an ancient Sears Roebuck black-and-white TV, which I had never gotten around to tossing out. Though it had once brought in CBS when it rained, there was now absolutely no picture—only the light cast by the electron tube. I laid the TV set on the floor, upending it so that the blank, lighted screen—slightly atilt the better to write upon—functioned as a backlighting source. On its surface, I placed the paper with the various Louise Brooks signatures; on top of this template, I put another of the blank canvases, through which I could now see the tracings as through the Hubble Telescope. Banjos up! Bending over the TV screen, I hunkered down with a magenta pencil in my hand. I breathed in and out athletically, making the kind of natural-birthing sounds I had hated when other people made them at the gym to which I could no longer afford to belong. Accompanied by a series of rapid exhalations, with the weathered paper atop the template, I ran the colored pencil over the signature . . . never stopping, continuing my HUH-HUH-HUHs, never lifting the writing instrument off the paper, and thereby eliminating all the stoppages and jitteries to which forgers' flesh is heir. My technique was a kind of riff on the actual signature, a tune played over the melody. And it worked fine. This is not to say that the loops and swirls were Euclidean—they were not. But it had to be taken into account that Louise was old. Louise was ill. Louise was a drunk. As it turned out, many of the major characters whose signatures I emulated fitted into at least one of these categories.

But it was the content, style, and humor that really sold the letters . . . that made me for a time the sensation of the raffish autograph business. And my success as a forger was somehow in sync with my erstwhile success as a biographer: I had for decades practiced a kind of merged identity with my subjects; to say I "channeled" is only a slight exaggeration. Novelist Rita Mae Brown observed in a review of *Kilgallen* that I found "heroes in middle-aged, quirky women . . . revealing, sometimes painfully, their personal struggle and shortcomings."

Faux Louise

*C*reating the phony Brooks letters started with baby steps. Still very unsure of myself, I cobbled together farragoes, taking paragraphs from several letters, then mixing and matching, changing the prose only slightly—"in the style of." I never duplicated word for word. (This was a matter of professional pride as a writer and because I imagined, in my mind's eye, an enormous dealers' bazaar at which the dealers perforce shmoozed with one another and compared merchandise.) I did, however, use certain verbatim sentences or phrases because they were just too good to be altered or excised. For instance, this is what Louise—the real Louise—wrote about the time the studio mogul Harry Cohn invited

her to his couch: "I would have burned in hell before sleeping with that fat-assed little Caesar. My cat has spit up hairballs more attractive than him." Her attitude toward her new post-Hollywood life: "I was never very comfortable being viewed as a victim. I would rather be thought of as in charge of my own destiny, even when the destiny leads to Rochester." Then there were phrases she used in many of her letters. "When the moon throws a rock at Kansas" was one I never really understood. When hell freezes over? No matter. The dealers all seemed to like the phrase so I salted it through my forgeries. "I could have jumped off my carpet" was another of Louise's sayings. I had the impression this meant jubilation—if not jubilation, at least better than "out the window." She sometimes ended letters to people who were invited to Rochester with "bring a gun." She hated a lot of people, her hatred epitomized in the line "I wouldn't fart in his direction."

In creating my faux Louise Brooks letters there was invention and embellishment, but as with all my creations, I did not play fast and loose with large truths. Here, for instance, is one of my own, another "Dear Dorothy," a name which like all of the addressees is a complete fiction, pulled right out of the air in my room-with-no-view.

7 North Goodman
Rochester NY 14605

Dear Dorothy .

I hope you haven't put anything of importance in the
post for me lately. Since and during my flu I have been
a bad girl, throwing away almost all of my mail. I have
been laid low since early April, surviving on light meals
and thriving on dear old DrJohnson. I roused myself only
to return a library book on which I owed 15cents. That was
my Kansas upbringing kicking up a disturbance.

When we had our power failure and I feared an enemy
attack it was Dr Johnson whose example got me through it.
I remembered his experience in the Hebrides. Storm-tossed
and cosmically imperiled, he lay down in the cabin with a
"warm grayhound" at his back. I grabbed my transistor radio,
at the time, and listened to a New York radio station.

I think we were both trying to think of Virginia
Cherrel. Does she sound right to you? I met her after she
finished CITY LIGHTS, a beautiful, fair-skinned and corn-fed
kid who had used her divorce settlement to come to Hollywood
in the first place. She loved telling stories about how
crazy she made Charlie during the filming. He fired her
many times but took her back because his initial vision of
the blind girl was indelible. He made her do forty takes,
but he got what he wanted. She had problems finding work
after that and finally settled on a marriage to Cary Grant.
That, too, proved a failure when she was finally fed up
sleeping in the middle...with Randolph Scott on the other
side. When I saw her the lasttime she was married to the
Earl of Jersey, looking rafishing and contemptuous. I
understand he finally threw her out on her arse.

Adolph Menjou outsmarted himself when he had one tremen-
dous hit and decided to be a super-star and a mogul, smarter
than all the Jews in Hollywood. His own vulgar economies
and an inability to keep his fly zipped made the liaison
with Kathryn inevitable. She brought him close to ruin,
carousing and losing his money on stock market tips from
manicurists. She had a moment in the sun when Marion Davies
decided that she was one of the girls Mr Hearst would look
at but not touch. For a time, she sat at their ranch making
clownish after-dinner speeches.

Don't get me wrong, I despise Hollywood, always did!

regards

Louise Brooks

The first paragraph is a kind of olio, cherry-picked from many of Louise's real letters. She had had the flu (and since this letter is undated, as were a vast majority of my letters, there could be no chronological *gotcha!*), and somewhere she mentioned owing 15 cents to her local library. The episode of the blackout night is covered in Louise's letter to Herman on November 10, 1965, a day after the actual and memorable northeastern blackout. Among other things, Louise had actually written: "Then I remembered that Dr. Johnson, during a terrible storm in the seas among the Hebrides, lay down in the cabin with a warm greyhound at his back, and composed himself for the worst . . . I composed myself in bed next to the warm radio and listened to ABC in New York."

The misspelling "Cherrel" (accurately "Cherrill") appeared in Louise's letter to Herman of June 13, 1966. Virginia Cherrill was an actress who appeared in films in the U.S. and Britain during the 1930s. She is best remembered for her portrayal of the blind girl in Charlie Chaplin's *City Lights*. Chaplin had had trouble getting the performance he wanted out of Cherrill. All of this I paraphrased based on Louise's own recounting and on a standard biography of Chaplin. Cherrill was later married to Cary Grant; Louise describes the sleeping arrangement with utter delight in her own letter. And I used some version of it in several of my forger-

7 North Goodman
Rochester NY 14607

Dear Flora

    Jesus, I got a kick out of seeing society news about
the awfully haut wedding of Walter Wanger's daughter to
Winston Guest's son. I slept with practically the entire
wedding party: fucked both the father of the bride and the
father of the groom. I spent a lot of time with Winston, son
of the Hon. Frederick Guest, an equerry of the Prince of Wales
(mother a Phipps out of Pittsburgh), He , Winston, had a bit
of everything up in his Sutton Place pleasure pad. He was
part Hemingway, part Kennedy. He killed, conquered, stuffed
everything--the beasts of the jungle, the beauties in Hollywood.
Among them, a fascinated Louise Brook. As for Walter, he was
a sweet, well-educated, gentle man when I knew him, and very
wise about every stage of my so-called career. It was he who
warned me that I was getting shop-worn and that if I stayed
in Hollywood any longer I'd become a prostitute.

    In any case, I could not have been any more shocked
when he shot Jennings Lang in the balls. I can't imagine anyone
going into a jealous rage about Joan Bennett. People were saying
at the time, because the fight took place in the MCA parking
lot, that they were really squabbling over a parking place, but
Joan's husband before Walter had attempted suicide at the thought
of Walter having her, so she must have something that the camera
doesn't catch. I've known her since we were both children
practically. She's from a from snobby theat-uh family and
she must be glowing at this match made in Palm Beach heaven.
I'm sure the polo ponies are going to get quite a work out.

    Finally, I got to see HELL'S ANGELS again. The film's
flying scenes remain matchless. A lot of bad acting, of course,
in the unfortunate style of the time, but Jean Harlow literally
glistens. I thought all through it of how compelling the
young Howard Hughes was --full of charm, energy, and passion
that was practically polymorphous perverse: for aviation, for
Kate Hepburn, for movies, for politics. I think addiction is
a terrible thing. It has always amazed me that a drug was
strong enough to fell his Leviathan life-force.

    If you are through with the still pics, I would like them
back, please.

           Regards

        Louise Brooks

ies. (I had already discovered that the scandalous pleased the dealers. A clucked tongue meant a better price.) I remained faithful to Louise's rendition of her meeting Cherrill on the street, but I blundered elsewhere. Louise wrote, "She married Cary Grant and left him because he always slept in the middle—Randolph Scott on the other side." For reasons best left unexamined, I put Cherrill in the middle. Which can happen when you screw with history.

She adored gossip and obviously read the newspaper. The boast repeated here in the "Dear Flora" letter about sleeping with "practically the entire wedding party" was something she actually had written to Herman. The references to Howard Hughes and Katharine Hepburn are based upon the sentiments that run through her real correspondence. Jean Harlow touched Louise, who thought her a particularly vulnerable victim of powerful Hollywood men. The joke about the parking space as casus belli of the Jennings Lang shoot-'em-up had been circulating around town at the time of the scandal.

Louise had converted to Roman Catholicism in 1953, and eleven years later abandoned the faith, becoming as passionate an apostate as she had been a devout. She referred to her flight from the Church to frame her distrust of all

7 N Goodman Street
Rochester NY 14607
11 November 1966

Dear Bill

    Your friend is not such a dolt after all. He is better than
most of the fools who write to me, calling themselves journalists.
He is aware of the disgusting myths of the film historians, whose
sole purpose in life seems to be as centurians, guarding the sleepy,
self-serving lies of the lard-assed Establishment. I did not
leave the lusty shake of the Church, with all its comforting
warrants, to prostrate myself on the shrine of St Bogart, who
with all his sexual magnificence was a woman-beater and bully.
I pay no attention to IDOLS; idolaters make me puke.

    I am knuckling down now and it would be better if you gave
my address out only after consulting me. I am a difficult old
woman who moved to this dullish community to be let alone. I
do everything in my power to discourage these nettlesome brats
who are constantly asking me to sit down and do their work for
them, recreating on their behalf the truth about a time and a
place they can never even hope to know--some of them, like
Hollis Alpert, becoming rich and famous writing about films
they can't even bother their asses to see. I wanted to puke
when he wrote that in LULU, as a result of Jack the Ripper's
mutilating me--"for the first time a sexual orgasm was filmed."
The first time was in TAGEBUCH. Alpert is a lazy journalistic
slut who never saw me in any film.

    I thought Shulman's book about Harlow would start a trend
of truth and integrity. He smashed some particularly obnoxious
plastic idols, including Louise B Mayer and Paul Bern. Shulman's
history was true and terrible, right down to the sheets in
Mayer's notorious beach house. But finally nothing that
breaks up the monopoly of time-honored bullshit can prevail.
I write as I do because I must--I tell my life through criticism.
Anyone in a position to know that everything I write is absolutely faithful to the truth is either dead or dying. Alas.

    What I am most lacking here, living among the flaccid
and unsuccessful, are people who can teach me . I
seldom go out anymore. There is only bad weather and locals
who make me want to jump off my carpet.

                Regards

                Louise
                Brooks

cultic, unreasoned sensibility, typical of which was her response to the cineastes' worship of Humphrey Bogart. In "Dear Bill," the reference to "St Bogart" comes from her famous essay "Humphrey and Bogart." Louise endowed Bogart with "sexual magnificence" in her own letter of October 15, 1966. She did believe that he had beaten his first wife, actress Helen Menken, and she asserted it on July 24, 1966, adding, "He never laid a hand on Lauren . . . she was bigger than he was." When Bacall was asked about Louise's various claims by biographer Barry Paris, she harrumphed, "Absolute garbage. A total lie . . . She was a little—I don't know, cuckoo."

Of the approximately four hundred fakes I wrote from April 1990 until the summer of 1991, only the Louise Brooks letters derived most essentially from actual letters. I stuck to basic biographical and emotional truths. If, say, a visit from Roddy McDowall is referenced, it is because I knew that Roddy McDowall was in fact coming to call. The same is true of her animosity toward the family she had left. And, despite her jeremiads and her political incorrectness— she referred to the enthusiasts who'd rediscovered her as "fanatical academic pansies"—her small success as a film writer delighted her, as did the new generation of cineastes who had rescued her from reclusive anonymity in Rochester.

* ı •

7 North Goodman
Rochester 7 NY
20 November

Dear Paul

　　Your friend Barry was absolutely accurate in his predicting
that Cheap Charlie would write a vulgar book for vulgar people and
one that is virtually guaranteed a place on the best-sellout list.
He is essentially, you see, a vulgar man who just happens to be
a genius. I have been so busy all these years defending him
I had really forgotten what he was really like and why I always
disliked him. The lies he tells about Paulette are understandable:
she was a btich in a ditch and he grew to hate her. Andhis
delinquencies with respect to Von Sternberg are also under-
stable (in Charlie's terms). But why did he omit Martha Raye
the door darling, always undervalued, was magnificent in VERDOUX.
I can see now why he skipped me those two months in New York
at the time GOLD RUSH opened in 1925. But why in heavens name
does he insist he was there only a week? Hardly time for the
scandal in Walter Wanger's apartment when Blythe Daly bit him,
or Jo Davidson's bust of him, or the adorable pictures taken
during that stay by Steichen.

　　I will never have any idea of who Charlie is or was, but
never before have I been so repulsed by his nature. All that
vanity, all those smitten babes knocking on his bedroom door,
all his cheap bids for attention. All he really had to do in
his biography was to present some small sincere and exegetic
appraisal of his talent --his glorious, magnificent, uniquely
lovely TALENT.

　　I would be fibbing if I didn't admit to you that my little
cult pleases me immensely. I have been getting fan mail from
young ones all over the world, some of whom never saw LULU,
otherw who yearn to see it again. And as I told Dorothy those
little pieces of mine deliver satisfaction that kicks like a
mule.

　　I'm glad you liked the upside-down cake. It is one of
my specialties. Don't expect any more telephone calls originating
from Rochester. It is impossible to manage on the Bill Paley
allowance. This is the winter of your dime!

Louise
Brooks

The letters imputed to all the other celebrities were based on biographical data gleaned from various sources. But the initial inspiration was always the discovery of an *ur*-letter that I came upon in my archival meanderings. I don't remember which particular letter drew me to Edna Ferber, but the ease with which I reckoned I could forge the signature— *"Ferb.,"* and sometimes *"Edna.,"* period after each—was a major selling point. My research on behalf of the letters was similar to the research I had done for years as a biographer, though far less exhaustive. The facts of Ferber letters were gleaned primarily from *Ferber,* the biography written by her niece Julie Gilbert, and from the autobiography *A Kind of Magic.* Both of these books describe Ferber's enchantment with the young film star James Dean, the stuff of which I used in "I'm happy, sweet Richard." (She typically buried her salutations in the body of the letter.) Dean had died in his Porsche Spyder the year before: "Poor Jimmy Dean!" she had written on August 26, 1956. "He has grown into a kind of dreadful cult. . . . And such brilliant talent, so winning and at the same time so terrible." I dated my faux Ferber based on the imminent opening of the film *Giant,* in which Dean was featured. I dated all of the Ferber letters because it seemed to me that the punctilious Pulitzer Prize winner would have probably dated even her shopping lists.

September 4
1956

I'm happy, sweet Richard, that you felt confortable
enough to have the matter out with me. I have been
known to err, you know, even in matters of "behavior"-
about which I am supposed to know something. You were
right though: I did misjudge her.

Don't miss GIANT. It is, even if I do say so myself,
a WONDERFUL movie. I cannot look at it again though,
I fear. Poor, lovely, touching Jimmy Dean! His
self-slaughter (and that's exactly what it was)
appalls me. I loved him deeply and he had no right
to be so dumb. He had such a gift of life and none
for surviving.

On the lot, you know, he rode me around in that
murderous car. What fun he was. Now a depressing
Cult burgeons, all about his death.

If we meet, if is best for me later and not earlier.

                    Yours

                    Edna.

Dorothy

Dorothy Parker's epistolary legacy is spare. In my forgeries, I was limited to the four years she spent in Hollywood in the early '60s because the *ur*-letter was headed with her Norma Place address. Happily, Marion Meade's definitive *Dorothy Parker: What Fresh Hell Is This?* covers those years extensively, from the spring of 1961 when Dorothy left the Hotel Volney in New York City, most reluctantly, to rejoin her husband, Alan Campbell, in Hollywood, through March 1965, after Alan's fatal drug overdose when she was escorted to the airport by Clement Brace and John Dall, with her foot pillow and her dog Troy in tow. There was good material for my letters during these years: Dorothy teaching at a local col-

DOROTHY PARKER
8983 NORMA PLACE
HOLLYWOOD, CALIFORNIA

Dear Joshua,

It was good to see you after eons,
if only for an afternoon. If Alan ever finishes
our guest wing, I will insist on your staying in
it, that is, of course, if we are not reduced to
turning it into a bed-and-breakfast affair with
the Campbells as local bonifaces. (Didn't she used
to write?) We might call it Hotel Hot Sheet or,
to encourage, people with fallible pets, Dot's
Doo-Drop Inn. This is a blue time really since
the movie with Marilyn is a definite abort.
They'll be no Good Soup in the can: no great
loss since the studio fucked it up royally.
We're waiting for work and collecting unemployment.

Goethe, the Hun writer, once said
that three weeks was all the fun he ever had in
his life, so it is most ungracious of me to complain.
But money is a problem. We are thinking of turning
"Big Blonde" into a board game. What do you think?

Yours,

Dorothy Parker

lege where none of her students knew who she was; she and Alan unemployed, pouring cheap scotch into Black Label bottles; Dorothy selling her review copies to secondhand book dealers. Brace and Dall were "the boys across the road," emblematic of the residents of Norma Place, a colorful lot, mostly borderline show business gays. Dall had actually been a big star, appearing opposite Bette Davis in *The Corn Is Green* and then in Hitchcock's *Rope*; his lover, Brace, had fallen from a modest plateau, in Dorothy's short-lived

DOROTHY PARKER
8983 NORMA PLACE
HOLLYWOOD, CALIFORNIA

Thanksgiving

Dear Joshua,
    Alan told me to write and apologize.
So I am doing that now, while he dresses for
our Turkey dinner with the boys across the road.
I have a hangover that is a real museum piece;
I'm sure then that I must have said something
terrible. To save me this kind of exertion in
the future, I am thinking of having little
letters runoff saying, "Can you ever forgive
me? Dorothy."
    Can you ever forgive me?

Dorothy,
Dorothy.

Ladies of the Corridor and as the original robot in *R.U.R.*
Composing this letter, I had no idea whether they'd actually
had Thanksgiving dinner with Dorothy and Alan. But it is
well within the realm of possibility.

The line "Can you ever forgive me?" is mine. As I wrote
it, I imagined the waiflike Dorothy Parker apologizing for
any one of countless improprieties, omissions, and/or cut-
ting bon mots . . . apologizing with no intention whatsoever
of mending her wayward ways.

The hangover line, like all of the best, is Dorothy's.

Noël

I had the most fun—too much fun, it would turn out—
playing with Noël Coward. We were on a first-name basis.
I signed only "Noël" because his complete signature—a flamboyant wraparound—was way beyond my elementary artis-
tic abilities. The swashbuckling *N* was a challenge to which I
brought various devices we used in high school geometry for
forming arcs. To no avail. I did the best I could freehand. The
dealers, nevertheless, clamored for more Coward. I remember
Anna Sosenko, who loved my stories about her euchred col-
leagues, scoffing at my roughneck *N*, claiming it never would
have passed muster with her. "Those idiots," she laughed.

The *ur*-letter of my Noël Coward oeuvre, from which I

learned his characteristic letter-writing habits—five spaces between sentences, indentions of thirteen spaces—was a short note he'd written to producer Cheryl Crawford, who was interested in producing one of his plays on Broadway. My faux letters were all done on his Montreux letterhead, one hundred of which I had had copied by one of my printers in the West Twenties. My database about his loves and hates and a thousand marvelous parties derived from the standard Coward biographies. But I drew overwhelmingly from *The Noël Coward Diaries*, edited by Graham Payne and Sheridan Morley, which brim with echt Noël Coward. He wrote this, for instance, about an event during a short hospital stay: "A strange woman with orange hair bounced into my room and asked if I was Miss Davis and if I would like a shampoo. I replied to both questions in the negative." The problem that he had been hospitalized for turned out to be gastritis, which he blamed on professional annoyances perpetrated by a bevy of professional annoyers. "I seem to be doomed," he sighed, "to sit patient and still, watching elderly actresses forgetting their lines." I loved his summing up after a first visit to Fire Island, "I wished really that I hadn't gone. Thousands of queer young men of all shapes and sizes camping about blatantly and carrying on—in my opinion—appallingly. Then there were all the lesbians glowering at each other. Among this welter of brazen perversion wander a few 'straights', with children and dogs."

I2th July 1964.

My dear Billy,

I enjoyed our talk tremendously
and I was not in the least upset by that
article. My professional demise has
been predicted gleefully for years now by
the same types who blame the Queen Mother
for their own dreary lives and meagre talents,
and who flock to see the soggy, turgid
maunderings of left-wing, often carbuncular
drones about whom even Ken Tynan has begun
to say 'Enough!' and 'Whither"? If they
only had good hearts and some humour, I
might more easily lend án ear, but any
intercourse at all with them leaves me
bored and inordinately depressed.

The Ahernes came to dine
on W dnesday and brought along Garbo.
We jointed Bobby Andrews at Adrianne's
for a lovely buffet.

Please do send those re-
cordings. My major problem is grammar,
especially verbs. For that, I must apply
not the ear but the arse.

Yours, ever,

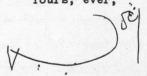

Sitting down with his diaries for inspiration and a British dictionary by my side to help with my "humours" and "cosys," I composed over time more than one hundred fifty letters that I attributed to Noël Coward. "My dear Billy" sprang from a multitude of screeds in the *Diaries* about the state of the British theater in the sixties and the angry young working-class playwrights, most notably Shelagh Delaney and John Osborne, whose work eluded and appalled Coward. I based the content and diction of my own letter on a Coward entry of September 26, 1960, in which he celebrates what he sees as the diminishing appeal of "the new movement," and the cooling enthusiasm toward it of critic Kenneth Tynan. The quotidian stuff about Garbo and the dinner party I rephrased from his account of July 9, 1964. The rest is invented minutiae. I sold the letter to a delighted dealer in Annandale, Virginia.

"Dearest Rob" went to a dealer in New Hampshire in November 1990. It was one of my favorites. My own line about Edna Ferber as unlikely twin was inspired by his anguish over the performance of Bea Lillie in a production, which he directed, of *High Spirits*: "Miss Lillie stumbles, flounders, forgets, remembers, drives the company mad and is as much like Madame Arcati as I am like Queen Victoria." All of the *Sound of Music* material I wrote was based on Coward's original critique of the musical: Mary Martin was too old,

LES AVANTS
sur **MONTREUX**

Sunday.

Dearest Rob,

You are among the first to know.
Bill was here and, in spite of my resolute
disapproval, they are going ahead with the
film about Gertie.   Julie Andrews is
set for the title role.   She is about as
much like Gertie as I am Edna Ferber's twin,
but what can one do!   I liked her athletic,
careering, whilom nun in 'The Sound of Music'.
She is a bright, talented actress and quite
attractive since she dealt with her monstrous
English over-bite.   It will be interesting -
more interesting, I hope, than dear Gertie's
actual life.

I am looking forward to seeing
Marlene.   The canny old Kraut remains one
of my most cherishedd friends.   This time,
however, I intend to talk to her briskly
about her predisposition to whining ad
nauseum about her ageing process, as though
she were the first gorgeous lady undone by
Father Time.   And I would dearly like to
teach her something about humour, as in <u>sense</u>
of humour.   Unteachable, I suspect.

Tell me more about Howard J.

Yours, and very much anticipating,

the lyrics "embarrassing," and the property, in general, "sawney and arch."

My "careering, whilom nun" was from Coward's "too many nuns careering about and crossing themselves and singing jaunty little songs." (Had I to do it over again, I would not have put that comma between *careering* and *whilom*.) The Marlene material was based on his running commentary throughout the *Diaries*, with regard especially to her resentment about growing old and her profound lack of humor. The last line, "Unteachable, I suspect," Coward might have written, but he did not.

These two letters were taken to be the real thing by editor Barry Day, a longtime student of Noël Coward's life, and included in *The Letters of Noël Coward*, published in 2007 by Knopf. The segment beginning "Julie . . . is about as much like Gertie as I am Edna Ferber's twin," and concluding, "more interesting, I hope, than dear Gertie's actual life," was used at the very end of the *Letters* as practically the eleven o'clock number. For me, this was a big hoot and a terrific compliment.

There were other letters, oddments occasioned by a lucky strike in the library, such as an old piece of blank stationery from the Algonquin Hotel, on which I typed a missive from

St. Bogart. I learned from my research that he stayed at the Algonquin when in New York City. I turned out a couple of George S. Kaufmans, who wrote two-sentence letters, and longer ones I imputed to Tennessee Williams. I discovered a batch of letters written by Clara Blandick, the actress who played Auntie Em in *The Wizard of Oz*. Blandick had had a bad end. Sick and impoverished, she swallowed pills and then swathed her head in a plastic bag. *Oz* stuff is prized among memorabilia enthusiasts; Clara Blandick's value has increased in proportion to the sadness of her leave-taking. An online auctioneer described her signature as "the Holy Grail of Oz autographs." Blandick, an easy forgery, became a minor canon in my collective works. Once I read that Bette Davis was in town and staying at the Lombardy, the chic residential hotel on New York's East Side. I had met Davis there when she and I were planning to put together her autobiography. Now I went to the Lombardy, sat down at their Louis-something, centrally located *secrétaire*, and pulled several pieces of Lombardy letterhead out of a drawer. As I pretended to be composing a letter, I slipped the luxe blank pages into my bag. "May I help you, madam?" an employee asked. "No, thank you. I worked with Bette Davis on her last book and I was going to write her a note, but I think I'll telephone instead." The fake Bette Davises did not fetch a good price, and I ended up using that creamy Lombardy paper for Scrabble scores.

The ten or so Lillian Hellmans I created were based on an actual letter to me, which I discovered in my files late in my criminal career. I'd written to her to request an interview for my Tallulah biography. Portraying the wicked Regina Giddens in Hellman's *The Little Foxes* had been the capstone of Tallulah's acting career and I wanted to talk to the playwright about that time. Not surprisingly, since a Hellman turndown is standard issue in the kit bag of American biography, she refused to cooperate. She was a difficult woman: happily, her signature was easy.

I rehashed her refusal letter in several of my own, this one to Cousin Sidney, all about her initial real-life rebuff of me. Sidney was used in my letters from time to time. I'd grown rather fond of him, and missed him since I had invented his move to London.

The undated faux has Lillian again turning Sidney down; here, in London, he has involved himself with a biography of Dorothy Parker. Mr. Ringrose and his book were made up, but the possessive and proprietary actions of Hellman toward Dorothy Parker were not. In her book

LILLIAN HELLMAN
630 PARK AVENUE
NEW YORK, N. Y. 10021

November 9, 1970

Dear Sidney:

I was sorry to have to say no once again. For personal reasons that you and I have discussed, I do not wish to cooperate in any biography of Tallulah. There are plenty of people who will tell her about this period. When she finds them, I have agreed to read over the section of the manuscript that concerns "The Little Foxes."

I did tell her that Tallulah did not do the movie because the producer wanted Bette Davis, and I did deny that I agreed to certain changes in the play because Tallulah insisted. I have no memory of her asking, and even if she had, I would not have allowed it.

I am feeling more and more like the wicked witch of the East. I suppose, after my period of canonization, it should have been expected. There is a tide in the affairs of men, but this is the decade of the illegal dump.

Come around and I will feed you.

Warmly,

Lillian Hellman

about Parker, Marion Meade writes, "Hellman's attitude toward her guardianship of Dorothy's and Dashiell Hammett's estates was essentially negative. As one of her biographers later noted, she did not encourage those 'who would like to keep books on Hammett and Parker, whose literary papers she keeps safely out of sight.' She refused to cooperate with anyone who wished to write about Dorothy."

With regard to "Dear Sidney," undated: there was no "Steve and Martha," but there was certainly a Vanessa Redgrave, brilliant as the Julia about whose provenance there was a storied dispute. Redgrave, a Trotskyite who paid dearly for her militancy, adored Hellman and read aloud to her when the writer was nearly blind toward the end of her life. And only weeks before her death, Hellman submitted an affidavit to the court defending Redgrave, who had been fired by the Boston Symphony with which she was to have performed.

LILLIAN HELLMAN
630 PARK AVENUE
NEW YORK, N. Y. 10021

Dear Sidney:

I have just finished writing to Mitch and Wyatt about ~~the~~ the Ringrose book. As we discussed, this is not the first biography of Dottie Parker that has been brought to my attention. Viking Press commissioned one by a man named John Keats several years back. They did not consult with me about the book, although four other publishers had asked for approval or suggestions.

I must stand by my first response. Dottie Parker never wanted an autobiography and did not wish to allow a biography. We did speak about the possibility and I gave her a promise when she was ill. I have, of course, even as the executrix, no legal right to forbid such an endeavor, but I have a moral obligation to tell you her wish and to say that I will certainly not see Mr. Ringrose. I thought you should know that.

I did finally look at the finished movie. I thought Jane and Vanessa extraordinary. I was no displeased except by the parts that made me look "butch tough" with a cigarette.

I have definite opinions about Vanessa, but she is no more anti-Jew than the rest of the English in her class.

I shall be in New York until the end of this month if you want to reach me, and after that I shall call you. Please say hello and warm regards to Steve and Martha. I thought they were a bright and attractive addition.

Affectionately,

Lillian Hellman

Sidney Brozen
17 South Hill Park
London NW
England

The Jig Is Up

I sold my bogus billets to perhaps thirty dealers nationwide. Some of the Noël Cowards went to a Swiss company. These autograph memorabilia merchants are a mixed bag, primarily men. Their ethical standard is set by the Professional Autograph Dealers Association (PADA), which obliges its members—though not all dealers are members—to warrant in perpetuity the authenticity of what they sell. Many of the people who bought from me did not seem to be scholars. Notable exceptions include David Lowenherz of Lion Heart Autographs, Naomi Hample of Argosy, both in New York, and especially Catherine Barnes, a Philadelphian with a Ph.D. in history from Columbia University. She was the only dealer who indicated to me that she had gone to some books to find out more about one of the characters referenced in what I recall was a Noël Coward letter, though the character was fictitious and was not obviously in anybody's index. Barnes purchased six Cowards at an extremely fair price. Her twelve-hundred-dollar check made it possible for me to begin some serious root canal torture. I never met her. She was just a cultured voice on the phone, and a nice check in the post.

The ambitious backstory I had made up about Sidney Brozen and his tormented sopranos turned out to have been a waste of creativity. Nobody asked me about Sidney, though I volunteered information about him from time to time. The dealers overall seemed spectacularly incurious.

In the early stages of my career as a literary forger, I had used rather good watermarked stationery for the letters of Coward, Ferber, and Hellman, all of whom were affluent and not averse to flaunting it. But watermarks are theoretically dateable. I found that out after a batch of Lillian Hellmans was returned to me without explanation by a West Coast dealer who had been very eager to buy the letters in the first place. Looking for an answer I contacted the paper's manufacturer, Eagle Bond, and determined that the paper had been made *after* the date I had emplaced on one of the letters. And

I resolved then to use only unmarked paper for all my letters, though I never determined that the watermark had been the culprit. Now I was worried that the absence of a watermark might impugn. But only one dealer, in my presence, actually held a letter up to the light for scrutiny. It happened to be another Hellman. Apparently knowing Hellman's reputation for sparing no expense (William Buckley once chided the left-leaning playwright on seeing her expensive suite of Mark Cross luggage that, he concluded, could have fed a village), the dealer voiced his puzzlement at the low-end paper, but then shrugged and said, as I exhaled, "She was probably out of stationery and ran some copies off. I've done that."

Once, one of the out-of-town dealers left a message asking me to telephone. Which I did immediately from a bar in Greenwich Village called Eighty-Eights. I always got right back to dealers. This was a function of my constant state of anxiety. On the telephone, he told me how "ecstatic" two of my Louise Brooks letters had made a schoolteacher customer of his. Chatting over the cabaret din in the background he went on about his pleasure, since his retirement, in dealing autographs and memorabilia. I casually asked what he had done before retiring. "Oh, I was an FBI guy," he said.

I met one of stars of the field only once—Charles Hamilton, who had written several books on his cleverness in detecting forgeries. The cover copy of *Great Forgers and Famous Fakes* claims, "Hamilton is the world's foremost authority on autographs . . . his expertise has enabled him to track down and help put in prison fourteen manuscript forgers and thieves. He lives in New York with his wife, Diane, and their four children." Among the many frauds Hamilton assisted in uncovering were the so-called Hitler diaries ("patent and obvious forgeries"). But neither he nor éminence grise Kenneth Rendell penetrated the hoax perpetrated by Mark W. Hoffman, author of the Mormon forgeries, which had fooled various members of the church hierarchy and cast doubt on the official version of Mormon history. Hoffman was finally convicted of the forgeries and of the murder of two people who had threatened to expose him. Hamilton, when interviewed at the time of Hoffman's trial, said, "Two murders are pedestrian crimes. But to fool me, to fool Ken Rendell, to fool the whole world, requires not only forgery but a packaging of himself . . . now we know he's more than he appeared to be."

I met with Charles Hamilton in his New York apartment. Pink-cheeked, a lot of white hair, seated opposite me on a couch with his wife, Diane, Hamilton looked and sounded like a Lutheran minister. I offered him one of the terrific Lillian Hellmans, one of several sounding the same themes, which read in part: "I did look at *Julia* finally . . . I thought Jane and Vanessa extraordinary. I was not displeased except

by the parts that had me looking 'butch tough' with a cigarette hanging out of my mouth." Hamilton offered me forty
dollars for it, far below the hundred dollars that I was com-
manding at this late stage in my career. I refused the offer
and left the apartment, wondering then, as I wonder now,
whether Hamilton was onto me and was offering the pid-
dling forty dollars in order to subject the letter to whatever
arsenal of sophisticated technology he may have had at his
disposal. If that were the case, however, I suspected that his
price would have been higher.

Naturally, it was the New York dealers whom I got to know
best. One became a friend. He was about sixty. With an amaz-
ing comb-over and an ancient, wheezing dachshund, he lived
in a tiny SoHo apartment with good wood and wingback
chairs. I saw him a few times a month to sell him some of my
best, many of which he then resold to other dealers. Once I was
invited to a small gathering at his apartment and I gave him
a copy of one of my own biographies. When he asked me to
autograph it, I signed "Margaret Mitchell." We all laughed.

It was he who first indicated that there might be something
brewing, that some doubt had been cast on the authenticity
of my letters. I remember him standing, reading to himself a
putative Dorothy Parker letter, laughing as I had never seen
him laugh, which is to say he was "chortling" out of control. I
was sitting in one of his wingbacks, sipping a scotch. He had

read my books and liked what he read. Now, over this Dorothy Parker letter, he shook his head and seemed to come to some consoling conclusion. "You're good," he said, "but you're not this good." I had the sense to take a sip of my drink and keep my mouth closed.

But more was said several weeks later when the dealer took me to dinner at an Italian restaurant in the East Thirties. The dinner was arranged in part to thank me for the healthy profits he was making from the sale of my stuff to other dealers. But there was more, none of it expressed with full-frontal forthrightness. "We're having a problem with the West Coast dealers," he said. One of the dealers out there had tried to sell some Noël Cowards to a man who had known Coward well—well enough to realize shrewdly that Coward would never have revealed so much in a letter, certainly not about his sexuality. Coward lived through a time when homosexuality was a jailing offense. The *Diaries* from which I took so much of my material included frequent gay references and innuendos. But his *Diaries* were published posthumously and at a time when the climate of acceptance was on the turn. I realized that my letters were discredited. For the California dealers now, my well was toxic.

We were finishing our dinner. I had a second Rémy served in a goblet that could have held a dozen yellow roses. My dining companion mentioned another New York dealer with whom he had apparently discussed my letters. I suspected that neither of the dealers was prepared to sacrifice the proven profitability of my work. He said, "They're real if we say they're real." The meal was heavy on obliquity. I made no outright confession though I was tempted to say, "Now you know, I am that good."

But the heat was on after that. At various memorabilia shows, one of the West Coast dealers went from booth to booth pointing at my letters and exclaiming "FAKE! FAKE! FAKE!" The venerable radio commentator Paul Harvey, whose show I heard accidentally one morning, said "Look for a shake-up very soon now in the autograph field." He had to mean me. The only other shake-up would come years later with the advent of bogus signatures on bats and balls. And then there would be an item in a column by Cindy Adams, apostrophizing Dick Cavett: "To collectors like Dick Cavett, who owns Louise Brooks memorabilia: A clutch of bogus celebrity letters—possibly (including) Dorothy Parker notes—may be around. Be careful!"

I was at the post office mailing "a clutch of bogus celebrity letters," when I checked my service and heard the chilly voice of Alan Weiner, owner of the Academy Bookstore in New York, and a dealer in autographs. Alan was a dark, nervous man in his late forties, with whom I had done a lot of business. During deals, we always sat on milk crates in the back of his store, schmoozing before getting down to money matters—Alan frequently talking about his health, or about Court TV. He had a bad case of psoriasis, perceptible on his wrists and forearms, exposed beneath his rolled-up sleeves. Alan had asked me if I would agree to sell him all of my Dorothy Parker letters. He wanted to "corner the market." I went home and typed about eight letters over two days of focused, intensive work. Alan was delighted with the result.

The voice on the phone in the post office suggested something other than delight. He wanted to meet me as soon as possible for a drink. We met later that day at the bar of a spacious restaurant near his store. We whispered though we were the only people there. Alan scratched and talked. He had been called to testify before a New York State grand jury, convening to target: Me. Alan maintained that his testimony against me could be critical. For five thousand dollars—the value to him of the letters he was holding—Alan told me he would not testify. I believed the part about the grand jury. I had no idea whether he could actually refuse to appear or to temper his testimony once there. This was no time, however, to cavil. I told him I was expecting a royalty check presently and that I could pay him upon receipt. This was a lie. I hadn't received royalties on any of the books for years. Would he give me time? He nodded, paid for his Coke and my scotch, and left. I finished my drink while cleaning up his psoriatic flakes with a cocktail napkin. The bartender came over to pick up his not-very-generous tip. "His wife found out about us," I whispered.

Violets for His Furs

About a month before this bad-news period began, I had received a stubby-penciled letter on cheap, lined paper with an odd return address. The first letter I had ever received from prison, it was from Jack Hock, my old bartending acquaintance whom I had kissed off several years previously. Jack was a tall, wheaten-haired gay man, then in his early forties, though he lied about his age all the time. He kept his good looks in spite of the many beatings he had received, his friends told me, from hustlers for whose services he had refused to pay. Jack had always managed to get himself repaired well, at bargain-basement prices. His teeth, for instance, were courtesy of a dental clinic connected with New York University. They were large and gorgeous, though so close together they made elegant dining difficult. (Think Steve Buscemi, toothpick in mouth, excavating his Clark Gable choppers.) He was a chain smoker and believed that the little stubby cigarette holder he fastened to the ends of cigarettes would keep him cancer-free. He often had a cigarette in one hand and a toothpick in the other. I don't think he knew about flossing; perhaps he just didn't believe in it. Jack was from somewhere in Pennsylvania Dutch country. His parents— the folks who raised him—were named Mildred and Floyd. Jack claimed, however, that his real mother was a Jewish psychoanalyst who had been forced to give him up. There was probably a poignant basis for the lie. Jack said he had spent some childhood time in the care of a famous pediatric sexologist named Dr. Money in a Baltimore hospital. He had perhaps attached himself to a staff psychiatrist.

Despite a touch of wayward charm, he was a grifter at heart, whom I had first met when my book *Kilgallen* was still a hot property. Jack had paid handsomely for the option rights; Floyd had given him the money to play producer after Jack was fired from his bartending job for stealing. (In fact, he was hoping also to assume one of the parts in the prospective biopic though his experience was limited to a fleeting nano-appearance years before as a sailor on shore leave in a Steve McQueen movie.) His current Hollywood excursion, staying at the priciest hotel in town, changing his name to Jack Hawk, had been a hoot and a half. Looking for a writer, he met with Paddy Chayefsky, who passed on the property, claiming he could not write dialogue for women (borne out, I think, by *Network*), and with Ernest Lehman. Jack came back without a writer, but with plenty of table talk. "So I said to Ernie, we can bring this movie in for under . . ." "Ernie? You called him Ernie?" "Sure, what's wrong with that?" "Did he say, 'Jackie, why don't you call me Ernie?' Jack looked perplexed. "No."

My agent at the time, Gloria Safier, was frequently queried about this odd, chain-smoking chap who was shopping *Kilgallen*. She too had picked up on his vagrant charm and began referring to him as my retarded younger brother.

Jack and I became friends. I called him Jacket. And tried to protect him from his other friends, most of whom weren't much smarter than he. I had to intercede, for instance, when he was in the hospital awaiting imminent surgery and one of his gang, hearing that he was not being fed, tried to sneak him a sandwich. On another occasion, when I was depressed about an affair that was looking hopeless, I sought sanctuary in his well-appointed Mitchell-Lama apartment, went to bed in his living room, and woke up to the sound of

Jack with a suddenly introduced third party—a trick he had found at two in the morning on Third Avenue. Jesus! I put my wallet under my pillow and went back to sleep.

And so it went, until I learned that Jack was continuing to shop my property long after his option was expired, having forged my name to an option extension (and misspelled it). Thunderous irony, of course, but I was appalled, and banished him as a friend for life, or so I thought. I lost track of him and I hadn't any idea that he was in jail, for armed robbery, charged with holding up a cabdriver at knifepoint after he had tried to grift his way out of paying the fare. According to the letter I received, he was soon to be on probation because he had contracted AIDS. He mentioned a telephone number at which he could be reached after his release. I straightaway phoned the number; a service answered and I left a message saying that I wanted to take him to lunch at The Ginger Man—the one near Lincoln Center—at 1 p.m. the next day. Jack was fifteen minutes late and breathless with excuses. For a guy just released from prison on account of mortal illness, he looked soigné in a white cashmere pullover and well-ironed jeans. Jack was the best ironer I had ever known, a masterly spray starcher—spray can in one hand, pant leg in the other, cigarette dangling out of the corner of his mouth, like a multitude of impoverished mothers in late 1940s movies preparing Linda Darnell for a first date with the local department store magnate. I suggested to him once that he think about opening a Chinese laundry.

At The Ginger Man, Jack spent some time proclaiming his innocence ("If I held that prick up with a knife, then where was the knife? They never found a knife!"). Then he cried tears because he hadn't been allowed to attend his father's funeral. Over BLTs, I told him the story of my life in crime so far. He put his hand to his mouth and kept it there—giggling the giggle that had probably alerted Floyd and Mildred to the fact that something about their adoptive *boychik* was just a little bit too *girlchick*. He was astounded by the idea of my being a forger.

Down to business, I said that I could no longer show my face around town, could not create another canon of forgeries, and that I needed five thousand dollars. I explained that this is where he came in. I was going to take a crook's tour of major university libraries, replicate some valuable letters in their various collections, and then replace the McCoy with forged copies. I would then give Jack the stolen originals to take around and sell to the New York dealers with whom I could no longer do business. Jack would get fifty percent minus my expenses. This cloning scam would be, I said, my second trimester. Jack sat for a minute, alternating toothpick and cigarette. "Do you want to do this thing with me?" I asked. Jack said, "Yeah. What's a trimester?"

Trimester Two

First, I altered an old Macmillan book contract, whiting out the date and the words AN UNTITLED BIOGRAPHY OF ESTEE LAUDER BY LEE ISRAEL, replacing those with A WORK PROVISIONALLY TITLED AUTHORS AND ALCOHOLISM—a rubric wide as a flight deck. I used the fiddled-with contract to gain admission to the Columbia University Division of Rare Books and Manuscripts, and then to the New York Public Library's Berg Collection. Each contained thousands of letters written by authors who drank. On my initial visits, I feigned note taking, but I was really surveilling the security system in place at the various libraries. The most threatening security element

remained the librarians, who issued a box full of correspondence and then checked its contents after it had been used.
I was satisfied that I could do this. What I had in mind to
do was not so original, though I had thought it up independently in the taxi after my last meeting with Alan Weiner.
Arriving in the library, I would request, say, a box of William
Faulkners, assessing then the feasibility of replication: paper
had to be plain, not personalized; letter had to be typed; the
signature easy. Walt Disney, for instance, would have been
out of the question: his signature looks like something underneath the Articles of Confederation.

I took the show on the road, visiting various libraries. There I would call up a box of letters, choose two or
three to my liking and copy them word for word, comma
for comma, noting spacing, indention, type, and paper size;
then, carefully—and this was when my heart thumped like a
bass fiddle in back of Barbara Cook—I traced the signature.
This was the part that could have attracted undue attention.
Once at Yale, I thought I saw someone studying me from
behind an unabridged *OED*. False alarm apparently. I never
did discover whether I was being scrutinized.

After I had done the initial copying I repaired to my
apartment, or to my hotel if I was out of town, and rep-
licated the letter. I didn't take my old TV with me on the
road, but I was usually able to find a substitute to use for

backlighting. I would return to the library the next day, request the same box, make the switch, and watch nervously as the librarian on duty counted and took—I was always happy to note—only a perfunctory look at the contents. I left the building after making a trip to the ladies' room, where I put the valuable pelf in my shoe.

Only once, at Princeton, did I come close to being caught. There, as at most archival libraries, readers are given boxes containing requested material. The box is returned on completing a day's work. This I had done after performing a switch, returning the clones and keeping the legitimate letters, which I then placed among the many papers I carried. I had not bothered to shoe the real letters because the security had seemed quite lax to me during my previous visits. On leaving the room, I faced the librarian on duty, a young Israeli woman, who had several times simply waved me past. This time, however, she asked to look through my papers, and seemed quite prepared to take some pains. As I stood in front of her, I went into high alert, calling on the oldest area of my brain—the part that worked overtime on the savannah, evading predation by camouflage. I turned myself into ZaSu Pitts, a nervous dervish, arms flapping, stuttering nonsense, and then spinning back to the seat from which I had come. "Oh, goodness," I dithered, "I forgot to copy the dates on the letters I read. I'd forget my head if it wasn't attached. What a dope I am!" And I slapped my face hard—moving from ZaSu Pitts to the more challenged of the Three Stooges. Looking concerned now about Lee Israel's sanity, the young Israeli walked over to me and put the box down on my table. I returned the real letters, withdrew the replications, and took about half an hour to feign work. Then I walked to the remotest reaches of the reading room and tucked the phony letters into some very recherché volume. I gathered my stuff together again, offering it to the alert Israeli for a look-see. She waved me away. Having witnessed my performance as both Curly and Larry, she must have thought me incapable of theft.

Between February and July 1992, I visited Yale's Beinecke Rare Book and Manuscript Library with its extraordinary Noguchi sculptures, Penn State, Syracuse, Cornell, back to Lincoln Center with its glorious collection of Hemingways written to producer Leland Hayward, Princeton, Harvard, and even the Hargrett Library in Athens, Georgia, which holds many of Margaret Mitchell's valuable letters (an easy signature and a great favorite with some collectors). The curator at Hargrett told me that Miss Mitchell did not have a drinking problem; I answered that I was also investigating the writers who had managed to maintain their sobriety in a field littered with cirrhotic livers.

I had begun to buy my old manuals from a store in the West Twenties that sold vintage machines. Soon my rented locker in an ugly tattooed building on Amsterdam Avenue—where I stored them all, stacked neatly over four wooden rows—began to look like a pawnshop with a mighty distinguished clientele. Royals, Adlers, Remingtons, Olympias, even a German model with an umlaut, which I had bought for Dorothy Parker, knowing that she would have fun with an umlaut. I attached individual hang-down tags to each, with the putative owners' names: Edna, Noël, Dorothy, Clara Blandick, Aldous Huxley, Louise Brooks, Eugene O'Neill, Kurt Weill, Bogart, Hellman.

Jack wouldn't tell me what kind of story he had cooked up to explain his possession of the letters he was selling, nor would he take any suggestions from me. It didn't matter anyway because he was succeeding. And he seemed happy with his new situation, pleased to move out of his SRO room into a decent apartment on West Seventy-second Street. Some welfare agency was paying his rent, and he was able to furnish his new place in his own good taste—a behemoth poster with Judy Garland in tramp makeup excepted. How he explained his new setup to his probation officer, he didn't tell me. But again, it apparently worked. He had found a book about pricing autographs and would say to me before embarking on a sale, "I think I'll ask . . ." His prices always seemed pretty high; however, he usually got what he asked for. My only suggestion to him about meeting with dealers was to try to avoid using the word *relevant*, one of the many he simply couldn't handle (his *nuclear* was a holocaust). One of Jack's best customers was Alan Weiner, who was buying his own silence.

I had allowed Jack to go out alone and do his deals and return to my apartment, where he would pay me half of what had been paid to him. But grifters' habits die hard. On returning one day after selling a couple of Margaret Mitchells to Weiner, Jack put down his Mark Cross folio, reached into his well-pressed pants pocket, and handed me $750, representing half of the $1,500 he claimed had been paid to him for the Mitchells. On a hunch, I asked to see the rest of his money. Always obedient because he was somewhat afraid of me, Jack pulled out $1,250, which together with my $750 would have added up to $2,000. "Alan paid me too much," Jack said with an anxious chuckle.

I had often watched Alan Weiner handle and count out money, when we both stood away from the milk crates in the back of his store and got down to business. The dealer counted and re-counted solemnly, his lips moving as though in prayer. He wasn't ever wrong. "I've seen Alan count money, Jack. He doesn't make mistakes." "Then I don't get it," my confederate replied, placing his hand on his forehead to indicate deep perplexity.

I *did* get it. And from that time on I accompanied him to his rounds, waiting in a nearby bar or restaurant, where he would meet me after the deal was done. Propinquity militated against Jack's natural inclinations, or at least gave him less time to screw around. Then we'd go back to my apartment to count.

And so it went, Jack hitting many of the New York dealers I had dealt with in the first trimester. He even found one on his own, a man operating out of Philadelphia. On a day trip to Philadelphia, Jack went on to Baltimore, where he uncharacteristically visited a library, discovering there a letter of Edgar Allan Poe's, worth maybe $14,000. He suggested now that I go and get it. I explained to him that the letter was too high-profile, too valuable, that it would invite super-scrutiny. He disagreed; I feared for a time that he would go after it himself.

One of the dealers with whom Jack had become chummy was a young, very amiable donnish man—the same chap who'd held the Lillian Hellman letter to the light. When the dealer told Jack he was about to be married, Jack gave him a dinner-for-two coupon to a restaurant. I was rattled when he told me about the gift. It was for a restaurant where Jack and I frequently dined. "Shmuck!" I said. "What if he walks in and sees us together?" "What are the odds?" Jack replied. ("What are the odds?" and "bottom line" used in situations having nothing to do with accountancy, as well as "this town" meaning heartless New York, were all favorite Jack locutions.) We never returned to that restaurant together.

I couldn't be as furious with my partner in crime as I had been back when I was an upright citizen. Jack's illness was progressing. He fell sick from time to time with AIDS-related ailments. Once he asked to take a nap in my apartment. (He lay on the floor because he hated my floral orange couch.) He fell asleep immediately. I felt his head, which was burning, awakened him and stuck a thermometer into his mouth. His temperature was 104. We went posthaste to the emergency room at St. Clare's—where he was admitted and kept for a week. It was a wintry day when I went to pick him up. He was dressed inappropriately. We passed a peddler selling cashmere scarves and I said that I wanted to buy him one. I put the scarf around his neck. "Violets for your furs," I said. "Huh?" Jack replied.

Come summer 1992, I felt that something was wrong. Jack had telephoned the dealer in Philadelphia and said he wanted to bring him more letters the next day. The dealer said that the following day was bad because he had a sister arriving in town, and he would get back to him. I had never encountered an autograph merchant who put visiting sisters over Ezra Pound. Could this be the beginning of the end? I had carried around a sack of worry since the birth of the scam—always at the back of my head. This Philadelphia episode put the generalized anxiety mode on higher alert. I thought a lot about serving time. I'd read Jean Harris's book about her experiences at the women's prison at Bedford Hills; her life there knocked around in my head, especially one guard's line to her, "This ain't no country club, Jean." Walking around New York, I was especially depressed by the sight of the Department of Correction buses . . . grim and filthy, chicken wire on the windows, specters out of John Steinbeck.

And I dreamt. I dreamt that I was sitting in one of the chicken-wire buses on my way upstate to prison. Noël Coward was driving the bus, and I was surrounded by the celebrity subjects of my forgeries, who were not on this occasion such good company: all nattering about how bad my typing was, how inept my punctuation. Dorothy Parker sniffed at my use of serial commas, which she compared to serial killers; Edna Ferber groused that the paper I'd purported to be hers had no watermark; Lillian Hellman blew out a string of expletives criticizing my prose rhythm; Louise said nothing except that she would not fart in my direction; and the sad-sad Clara Blandick lamented that the worst thing about being dead is that you couldn't kill yourself. Noël wore elegant evening wear, shifted the gears in anger, and spoke only once, his gaze catching me through the rearview mirror: "Imitation is not flattering in the least; it is the refuge of the third-rate. I'm thrilled that a friend of mine was savvy enough to have helped put you where you belong—among people rather below you in class who make vulgar noises ceaselessly, who will ridicule you for what they'll see as your grand ways—where the toilets are lidless and where government cheese—which is said to be more constipating than codeine—is served with abandon at every deplorable meal. You are getting, dear girl, precisely what you deserve. I'm only sorry that those imbecile dealers didn't nab you after the first look at your infinitely pathetic, spastic attempt to replicate my glorious and quite Euclidean initial N." He downshifted with asperity. I awoke in a funk.

This Ain't No Country Club, Lee

*I*t continued to be our modus operandi. Jack would make the sale and then meet me at an appointed restaurant or bar, then to my house to count the money. The sales hardly ever took more than half an hour, especially now that Jack was known to the dealers. Once he took more than an hour to meet me, and I joked, "Thought you'd run into the FBI."

On July 27, 1992, noonish, I waited at a fancy kosher deli while my partner made a sales stop by appointment. It was ten minutes before I was seated, and another fifteen or so eating coleslaw out of a petri dish before a harried waitress appeared. I ordered pastrami on rye, which took a while to arrive. I ate. I'd been there more than an hour, stressed out and literally chewing the fat, when it occurred to me that Jack had probably misunderstood and gone directly from the dealer to my apartment. I got the check and planned to return home, where I hoped Jack was waiting for me.

I left the deli, hooding my eyes from the sun as I searched for my sunglasses, and was about to put them on—when a man, who'd been walking west fast, stopped very abruptly. I can still hear the braking *shush* of his shoe on the pavement. He called "Lee" as not quite a question. A native New Yorker, I encounter people all the time whom I cannot immediately place. But I knew then that I had *never* in my life set eyes on this man or the man who appeared to be with him—one was in my face, the other hung back. They were both short, both in natty suits fitting too snugly around the chest, and knotted ties. The man in my face showed me a big star affixed to his wallet that glinted in the sunlight. The lunch-hour crowd milled around us. I was full-face in a comic-book panel.

I've spent my life in a state of high anxiety, waiting for the Cossacks. I am always worried. When one cause of worry exits my skull it is replaced immediately by another. They meet shoulder to shoulder, one entering, the other exiting the cave leading to my tympanic membrane. So the din that had been created by my knowing that the dealers were onto me had not been a whole lot different from the time in high school when I hadn't studied for a Spanish test; the worry over discovery, moreover, was assuaged by the fact that I thought the dealers would eschew any action that might bring publicity to their murky trade. But the appearance of the FBI agents made a difference. They were incarnational. Pushed my nagging warts into metastasizing tumors, turned my minor-key motif into a symphonic roar.

"We'd like to talk to you," said the Ed Harris type, clearly in charge, looking over the jamming traffic for a more isolated spot. We crossed the street south. He told me that they had collared Jack as he arrived at the shop of one of the dealers who had become a cooperating witness in their ongoing investigation. The agent repeated to me what Jack had just told him, names of colleges primarily. This is of course a traditional technique, stressing the hopelessness of denying what is already known. There were, disappointingly, no Miranda warnings because I was not being arrested. Neither had Jack been arrested. The agent now tried to draw me into conversation, but I was lawyer-savvy. His mind seemed to be a lot on what he had promised Jack. "Mr. Hock has requested that you not try to reach or telephone or harass him in any way." Sonofabitch Jack had been worked over by aggrieved tricks who'd blackened his eyes and broken his nose and kicked away his old teeth. But he was afraid of my mouth.

I left the agents and bought an enormous bottle of scotch, out of which, back at my apartment, I drank directly . . . while, hands shaking, I scissor-shredded pounds of research notes and the unused stationery of Noël, Lillian, Edna, Mrs. Parker, et al. I put the shredded paper into multiple Hefty bags. Running up the back stairs of my eighteen-story prewar apartment house, taking the steps three at a time—like a child, only panting—I dropped the individual bags alongside the garbage of sundry neighbors. Then I hied over to my mildewed locker—accessible by a whining and painfully slow industrial elevator—and woke up my gang of typewriters. I deposited them, one by one, in trash cans along a mile stretch of Amsterdam Avenue, watching the traffic to see if I was being surveilled.

Most of the old machines had been purchased at a hardware store on Broadway. After I had bought several of them, Mr. Farber, the owner, got up the nerve to ask me what I did with all the typewriters. I said kiddingly that I gave them to the homeless, a joke that now contained some truth, as they lay separately, their fates undecided, in wire receptacles up and down the Upper West Side.

I returned to my apartment, where I was "between beds." So I lay on a bare mattress in the living room. I dragged on the scotch bottle and planned a fugitive's flight to Fort Lauderdale, where my elderly mother and her husband lived, each beginning separate descents into senility. *I would disappear from here. I would live with them in their retirement community, where the old men jingled pocket change while standing in line for a four p.m. early-bird seating. I'd hide in their cheesy bedroom closet, coming out for pot roast and an occasional swim.* Made good sense to me as I lay there.

It had been one of the dealers who made the first call to the FBI, and it was another dealer alerted to an imminent sales visit by Jack at whose shop the agents had nabbed my flaky confederate. The first dealer had become suspicious of some of the letters Jack sold to him, all stolen by me from Columbia, which I visited frequently. I wasn't surprised; he was one of the few in his field who I suspected knew that provenance was not the capital of Rhode Island. The two FBI agents were actually in his office when Jack telephoned to tell him that he had an Edna St. Vincent Millay, a Jerome Kern, and a Thomas Wolfe. It was July 17, 1992. A meeting was set up with Jack for July 21. The dealer agreed to wear a wire. The agents followed Jack after he left the dealer's office on July 21 and noted his meeting with me at an enormous tourist trap of a bar in the big toe of the Empire State Building, where I was sitting and sipping a Tanqueray martini. Per FBI report: "Hock was observed meeting and conversing with LEONORE ISRAEL. The defendant was later observed boarding a subway train with Israel."

Developing the case against me was like shooting fish in a barrel, as I had known all along it would be. On every trip to any of the libraries I had to identify myself. I suppose I could have used false documents except that (1) it had never occurred to me, and (2) I wouldn't have known how to get them. This is a sample of the evidence used by the government: "On July 22, 1992, investigating agents spoke with the Assistant Librarian for Manuscripts at Butler Library. . . . He confirmed that the letters sold to CW-1 did belong to Columbia and that forged copies of these letters were now in the files." (CW-1 was FBI parlance for Cooperating Witness One: the dealer in this case who had first dropped a dime on me and my partner the rocket scientist.) The reports contained similar narratives about the other libraries I had visited.

Jack and I received subpoenas separately. I was directed to produce documents for a federal grand jury. There was absolutely no more contact between us now. The earlier state grand jury with which Alan Weiner had threatened me had never, for some reason, convened, though I did pay him incrementally the $5,000 he had demanded of me. (The money that I used to pay Weiner I obtained from the money Weiner was paying Jack for the letters I'd stolen from the various libraries which, it occurs to me, made Alan Weiner a sort of tertiary co-conspirator or, at the very least, a blackmailing patsy.) The two FBI agents, Ed Harris and Tonto, rang my bell that same evening after the meeting outside the pastrami palace and served me with a subpoena to produce documents to a federal grand jury appearance on the last day of July. The subpoena commanded me not to destroy any evidence, which was no problem since all of the evidence I could get my hands on had already been destroyed or, at least, scattered.

One of the documents associated with this period describes the agents' visit to my apartment: "Served subpoena at approximately 6:00 p.m. Lee was at home and had been drinking scotch." Correct. Lee was at home, and quite alone. I had maintained only casual friendships throughout my crime wave—and not too many of those. I had a mother in Florida and a stepfather; there was no way I was going to tell them how their best-selling author was paying her rent. I had a brother with whom I had never had much in common. Two wealthy and terrific gay men, a couple, Mark Upton and Coby Britton, were among the only outsiders in whom I confided. Coby had come into his considerable money through a forebear, the notorious power broker Mark Hanna, a turn-of-the-century Karl Rove. The descendants of Hanna, lucky Coby among them, owned most of Cleveland. I told Coby and Mark about my celebrity forgeries early in the undertaking. The three of us were lounging around their enormous blue pool in horsy Bernardsville, New Jersey, as one of Malcolm Forbes's beautiful giant balloons wafted overhead. We had a great, laughing time with Trimester 1. Mark was so amused he turned down Betty Hutton's "Pistol Packin' Mama" to give my story his full attention. I can't recall whether I told them about the letters stolen from universities. Coby was a Yale graduate and a Fulbright Scholar, and I didn't know how my intellectual banditry would have sat with him. Whether I made full disclosure or not, I did notice in a future visit that the framed, handwritten letter of Virginia Woolf's, once displayed in a cove underneath a staircase, had been removed.

I began attorney shopping now. I stupidly surmised that I was owed talented pro bono representation, having written extensively for *Ms.* magazine and been associated in the past with civil rights causes. Ridiculous, of course. But I was in a protracted breakdown of sorts. I went first to see the formidable black feminist attorney Flo Kennedy, to whom I had spoken once at a party and with whom I had dined at an uptown Cantonese restaurant. She did not take the case. "Honey," she said, "I'm old. I'm tired. And I'm going to Hawaii any minute."

Another attorney saw the case as an opportunity to take a tandem media ride: best-selling author forced into life of crime to save cat's life. He asked me straightaway to think about making a list of everyone I knew in the media. Then told me that I could get ten years for my crimes but that there might be mitigating circumstances. Was I going through menopause? Yes. That was going to be our defense. Temporary estrogen deprivation. Best-selling author undone by radical hormonal tumult. Don't you hear us knocking, Sally Jessy?

When I came to my senses, I found a lawyer through the Federal Defenders Program. He was a smart, handsome, young Orthodox Jew named Lloyd Epstein. When I called him from a street phone he asked me to come right over. There was never any plea considered by either of us but guilty. And he was incredulous that an attorney had told me that I was looking at ten years. I might conceivably get a year and change. "Oh, my God," I said. "You'll bring a book," Lloyd counseled.

Many of the things I feared never happened to me. These were mostly dignity issues. My crime, in lawyers' talk, was a sexy crime. That meant no drugs, no violence—intellectual shadings, literary stuff. I was a white defendant without a record who had written books. Nobody treated me disrespectfully on the federal level. I was never arrested, nor made to do a perp walk, nor put into a cell, nor manacled. The assistant United States Attorney assigned to my case was a thin, chic Asian woman. During our first face-to-face, I told her about why I had begun Trimester 1. She had to hear it, but the feds were interested only in Trimester 2: conspiracy to transport stolen property in interstate commerce, a class D felony. After our first session, Katherine Choo looked at the small watch on her thin wrist and said, "How about eleven-ish tomorrow?"

I was making no sense at all. I was crazed by the prospect of doing *any* time in jail. Nevertheless, drunk, unable to sleep, and flat broke again, I shoplifted a $3.95 bottle of Sominex from a local Price Wise, and I was taken away handcuffed in a squad car. I made myself perfectly obnoxious by correcting the cops' grammar on the trip to the station house. Once there, a hunt-and-peck policeman typing up the lengthy particulars of my looting muttered, "Three ninety-five! Three ninety-five!" as though he was diminished by the small-timiness of me. And now I *was* put into a cell where I languished for several hours; a policewoman escorted me to the door, after asking a sergeant, "Is this a keeper?" Twice I had to stand in a long line in front of the criminal court building in lower Manhattan waiting for a hearing that never transpired because the store finally did not show and charges were automatically dropped. A break for me! Judges do not look kindly upon crimes committed in the thick of another prosecution. My judicial virginity was still intact.

While I was awaiting my court date, I was taking a stroll through a part of Manhattan Island that had never gotten over Edith Wharton. And passed a shop with autographed letters in the window. I went in, and just for the hell of it, asked an amiable clerk if he had "something in a Dorothy Parker." He put one of my creations tenderly on an easel-like structure. It was a forgery that I had sold originally to another dealer for less than $100; and it included a favorite line of mine about Estelle Winwood, "the oldest living thespian," and her birds. This one was priced unframed at $2,500! There was a second Parker of mine also going for $2,500. The clerk gave me a tear sheet from the dealer's most recent catalog that pictured and then commented upon the second letter, describing it as written on Dorothy Parker's "personal imprinted stationery to Alex. Pure Parker." Delighted as I was at my letter's being experienced as Parker pure, I was nettled. I was going on trial as people were still making a great deal of money from the fruits of my labor. The extreme markups, which I'd not been aware of until this time, also annoyed me. Since the autograph business is gossipy and incestuous, I wondered how any dealer could not have known about the spurious pedigree of the letters.

DOROTHY PARKER
8983 NORMA PLACE
HOLLYWOOD, CALIFORNIA

Dear Germaine,

      I'm glad you liked the piece.
I am heartened because your taste is usually
so good.

      The ecnlosed is a "chain letter".
It presented a great dilemma to me because most
of my friends are dead. I am also including
the pictures you wanted. The woman by the piano
is Estelle Winwood, the oldest living thespian.
She has birds, which has always struck me as
oddly redundant.

      Alan sends hugs.

    Yours,

Dorothy Parker

I left the shop telling the clerk that I would be talking the purchase over with my husband, and later wrote a letter to the offending dealer on Dorothy's "personal imprinted stationery." The letter, signed "Dorothy Parker," chides him for his avarice. ("Poor wayward Lee Israel received only eighty-five dollars a pop when she sold them originally . . . Was it Proudon who said all property was theft? Or was that Ruth Chatterton during a violent political spat with Adolphe Menjou?") When I mailed the letter, Dorothy had been dead for more than twenty years. The letters were removed promptly from the dealer's inventory.

Prep Time

*B*efore my court date, I did the usual bullshit . . . voluntary community service, as impressive to the Court as discovering Jesus as personal Lord and Savior. I worked at the Museum of Natural History helping to prepare a new manual for their guides. Meanwhile, my lawyer, Lloyd Epstein, was doing a marvelous job bringing the numbers down on the federal sentencing guidelines, writing letters to the Court stressing my distinguished past and the badness of the patch that had driven me into a life of crime. They were heartfelt letters and not, I think, typical of the activities of an attorney working for scale. Apropos these guidelines, whose parameters include consideration of hegemony (was the defendant a leader or a follower? One of the few instances in American life where leadership is penalized), Lloyd wrested from me truths whose significance I had not realized, such as the fact that Jack was not just a pawn of mine but had set prices and made some of his own contacts. Lloyd was able to whittle down my numbers, so that the judge could—if he or she chose—place me on probation with no jail time. I drew federal judge Robert W. Sweet. Lloyd and I joked about the fact that Sweet had gone to Yale, one of the institutions I had hit hard, but I was heartened by Judge Sweet's résumé; he was a respected jurist who had spoken out against the draconian and inflexible laws applied in the so-called war on drugs.

On the day of my plea, I arrived in court gasping for breath. I had taken the subway, entering on West Seventy-ninth Street, bound for the Fulton Street stop way downtown. And I'd given myself plenty of time. I don't remember what I thought about on the train. I had done the jail scenario so often that it was completely played out on a conscious level. The rutted road in my cortex could no longer offer traction to these thoughts. I think I was experiencing instead some kind of *hum* from the older back of my brain . . . the hum chewing over the horror of imprisonment . . . out of earshot, maybe in Yiddish so as not to upset me. How I felt was numb, with a hum. I missed the Fulton Street stop, had to detrain and then go over to the uptown side. In New York City, subways are built like cata-combs; there is almost never a simple crossover route, but rather a subterranean walk, directed by arrows, that takes one up the stairs, then down other stairs, around and down and up again. And it is always damp no matter the season. I ran, cursing the signs, cursing the steps, misreading the arrows, then getting on the wrong train again, where I was stared at as I muttered, sotto voce, fuckitfuckitfuckitfuck—not apparently sotto voce enough. A baby stared at me and pointed. I was about to say, "What are you looking at, you little shit?" But I did not. Its mother was very large and also staring. I was breathless from the run, and sweating from places I didn't know I could sweat from.

Withal and miraculously, I arrived on time for my court appearance. Nobody was there with me as I stood before Judge Sweet, except Lloyd and his younger assistant. The proceedings were all very decorous . . . and undramatic, and so quiet. Quiet as it had once been when I'd come close to drowning in the lapping, serene Caribbean, before the cap-tain of my chartered boat dived and rescued me. Was I now to be pulled to safety by sweet Sweet?

The transcript is short. Judge Sweet asked me if in the last twenty hours I had used drugs, pills, alcohol—anything that would affect my ability to understand what was going on. I said, "I had a little white wine with dinner last night."

(In fact, I had had a lot more than a little wine that night and no dinner at all.) I meant more than half of what I told him, but my sentiments regarding Trimester 2, the thefts of letters, were straight as an arrow. "I feel and have felt over the past year enormous guilt and anxiety. I feel that I have betrayed really my community of scholars, a citadel of culture . . ."

I drew the Get Out of Jail card. Judge Sweet told me that he never wanted to see me again "in this context" (not a total rejection). I was sentenced to five years on probation, six months' house arrest. I was not braceleted because a home phone was needed for that, and I had once again lost my service. I wasn't to leave the state or consort with felons; I was to pay restitution within my means. I was directed to attend AA meetings, which I never did, though on my way to Julius', my favorite West Village bar, I regularly passed by a chapter of AA, at whose door my lapsed friend Elaine, fated to die in a Good Friday car accident, had regularly every Sunday on her way to work boisterously brandished the keys with which she was about to open her saloon.

The worst part of the house-arrest deal was the regular, early-morning invasions by two probation officers, who looked around my sleepy apartment for evidence of malfeasance. One of them once spotted an empty bottle of beer and asked me to explain. In fact, I had hidden the bottle in plain sight just to get a rise out of the sonofabitch. "That was drunk last night, Sherlock, by my friend . . . er . . . Irma." He hated it when I called him Sherlock. I told him—and I wrote to the Court—that I would address him properly when he stopped calling me by my first name. It was agreed.

This period was followed by four and a half years of probation. Because of this country's obsession with mind-altering substances—alcohol not included, nor the book of Revelation—I traveled downtown once a week, then once every two weeks, then once a month, to pee into a cup in a bathroom where the seat was always up, and to consort unavoidably with felons. There was often a wait to see an officer, during which I either read or counted the number of times my fellow felons said *motha fucka.* I got bored with this and went on to count *this nigga, that nigga,* and the vocative *Hey, nigga!* I would have doubtless been beaten to death in prison.

Jack, who had been sentenced to three years' probation, died in October 1994. He was forty-seven. I had encountered him only once after my day in court, when I was waiting to be called at a medical clinic. He passed right in front of me on crutches, having apparently broken a leg. He did not see me. I smiled at the thought of extending my leg and tripping him. There was an upside to his dying when he did, while he was free and looked after with love by members of the Gay Men's Health Crisis. His legal records indicate that he was at liberty only because certain papers had not yet reached the right desk. A revolver was somehow found in his possession, strictly forbidden to felons. Had he not died when he did he might have spent his last days in a prison hospital. I telephoned him once, near the end, and I could hear the rattling ravages over the phone. I'm not sure that he knew who I was.

My Third Trimester

·

W hat I told Judge Sweet about the guilt I experienced on account of my second trimester, stealing from cultural citadels, was somewhat overripe but heartfelt. I had spent a good deal of my professional life hunting and gathering in annals and archives, and messing with those citadels was unequivocally and big-time wrong, deserving of a dirty-bus ride with a railing Noël Coward.

I suffered and I paid by being barred from the libraries that I had plundered. An all-points bulletin was issued by Ex Libris, an archivists' group, alerting all to my misdeeds, and it remains looming in cyberspace to this day: "Lenore Israel has been sentenced for the thefts of modern manuscripts from rare books and academic libraries. Her modus operandi was to replace originals with high quality forgeries." After several years of keeping my distance, however, I thought it might be safe to return to the lower level of the Library for the Performing Arts at Lincoln Center, a nonsecure public space where readers are permitted to browse and borrow books about the arts. I was reading a biography of George Cukor when a guard appeared, searched my papers, and escorted me out the door, under the satisfied and watchful eye of the burly box boy who had once foraged resentfully on my behalf.

My guilt over the original thefts is mitigated somewhat by the gathering in of the epistolary diaspora. I cooperated with the FBI, and the real letters of the drunken American writers were so far as I know all recovered and returned safely to their archival homes.

I have never experienced strong qualms about my first trimester. The forged letters were larky and fun and totally cool. Parodies of icons—Coward, Ferber, Mrs. Parker, Louise, Lillian Hellman, and poor Clara Blandick. They totaled approximately 100,000 words, give or take. A quantitation falling somewhere between *Madame Bovary* and *Madame X*—not bad for less than two years' work. I still consider the letters to be my best work. Reminiscent of Dustin Hoffman's summing up in *Tootsie,* I was a better writer as a forger than I had ever been as a writer. Any remorse I experience about this phase of my life in crime has nothing to do with the money various dealers might have lost; I think most of the dealers came out ahead. The remorse here is personal. I betrayed some people whom I had grown to like. With whom I'd made jokes and broke bread. And in doing so I joined, to my dismay, the great global souk, a marketplace of bad company and bad faith.

Not too long after house arrest was done, and still in my probationary period, I found a staff position copyediting the venerable classroom magazines at Scholastic, the Spring Byington of the publishing world. I had not had to risk revealing my felon's identity because I started there as a freelancer, thereby sidestepping the rigors of the standard employment application. Six sufferable years passed, and while it lasted I learned a lot about *Tyrannosaurus rex* (capital *T*, small *r*) and how third graders in Mumbai (formerly Bombay) celebrate Diwali. Scholastic offered a more or less civilized environment, a decent salary, and appealing benefits . . . benefits that included veterinary insurance for darling Tallulah and Tennessee, calico and orange tabby, respectively, the current generation of my cats in residence.

Lee Braul

Acknowledgments

I am so indebted to producer David Yarnell, who at an overrated Chinese restaurant in the West Seventies listened first to this tale and encouraged me to write it down. And to Byron Dobell, who read it and laughed and set the book in motion to Stacy Schiff, Geri Thoma, Jeffrey Frank, and Sarah Hochman.

I am grateful as well to friend and researcher Ray Barr. He did latter-day face time at the library for me, so I was spared having to dust off my burka.

About the Author

Lee Israel was a biographer and copy editor who lived in Manhattan, west of Zabar's. She died in 2014.